A Little Silver Trumpet

A Little Silver Trumpet

THEA BENNETT

illustrated by Priscilla Lamont

BRITISH BROADCASTING CORPORATION

A Little Silver Trumpet was first shown on BBC1 in autumn 1980, with Siobhan O'Carroll as Alison Jessop and Ian Land as Johnnie Cleaver. It was directed by Dorothea Brooking and produced by Anna Home. The television adaptation by Julia Jones was taken from the original novel by L. T. Meade, first published in 1885. This book is based on the television series.

Published by the
British Broadcasting Corporation
35 Marylebone High Street
London W1M 4AA

First published 1980
ISBN 0 563 17884 1

Printed and bound in Great Britain
by W & J Mackay Limited, Chatham

Introduction

A Little Silver Trumpet by L. T. Meade was first published in 1885. Elizabeth Thomasina Meade was born in 1854 and was one of the most prolific writers for children in the late-nineteenth, early-twentieth centuries. She was the first person to write school stories for girls as well as a wide range of other novels.

She died in 1914 and her books are little known today. *A Little Silver Trumpet* was brought to our attention by Miss Helen Garnett of Clitheroe who is now in her eighties. She sent us her own precious copy of the book wondering whether it would adapt for television. We liked the book very much and although in its original form it contained much material irrelevant to a modern audience, the story and the characters emerged very strongly.

We therefore commissioned a television dramatisation of the book from Julia Jones, a well-known adapter, and this new version of the novel by Thea Bennett is based on her scripts.

We hope very much that a new generation of readers will enjoy *A Little Silver Trumpet* as much as Miss Garnett and her contemporaries did.

Anna Home

Chapter One

Oh, the sea was wonderful! Alison loved it. She ran by the edge, the wind tugging at her skirt and trying to snatch her woolly tam-o'-shanter hat from her head. Above her in the grey sky, seagulls wheeled and plunged towards the sea, crying "Kaa! Kaa!"

Beside her, big waves broke one after the other on the beach and slid back again, hissing over the pebbles. Day after day they bore strange objects to the beach and left them stranded there, high and dry. There were lumps of driftwood, glistening bunches of brown seaweed, and fragments of broken bottles worn smooth by the sea. Alison ran on, her button boots slipping and sliding over the wet shingle. Suddenly a great wave came crashing down, and before she could dodge out of the way, the long tongue of foam had lapped right up to her feet. She jumped back, and then knelt down to wipe the water from her boots. She would get a scolding if she went home with wet feet, for her mother had told her many times that salt water would spoil the leather.

Then she saw, nestling among the pebbles at her feet, a large curling shell. It was mottled with purple, and the curved inside was smooth and white. It was very big. She had never seen a shell quite like it before. She picked it up, brushed off some grains of sand, and put it to her ear. From deep inside she heard the sound of surging waves, and she covered her other ear with her hand to listen.

Behind her, high up on the strand, stood a small cottage. The roof was low, and the windows were small. It crouched on the edge of the shingle as if it were trying to hide from the wild weather.

Suddenly, a faint cry was heard over the noise of the gulls. It came again, and though the sound was snatched away by the wind, Alison knew it was her mother calling.

She started to run towards the cottage. Her skirts ballooned around her like a ship's sails, and she spread out her arms and let the wind carry her up the beach.

"Alison – you are a great silly girl!" cried her mother, who was standing at the door. She laughed as her daughter pushed through the gate, almost knocking her over, and stood panting beside her.

"Is it – is it time yet, Mammy?" asked Alison, breathlessly.

Her mother smiled. She had a kind face, reddened by the wind, and when she smiled it creased up into laughter lines, as if she were someone who was used to smiling a lot. She spoke with a soft West Country accent. "Is it time? Of course it's time! His ship docked hours ago, and he's always one of the first off."

Alison caught her breath anxiously. Her father was expected home that day. Mr Jessop was a sailor, the bosun on a large ship, in charge of many men. He had been away for two long years. What if she had missed him, and he had arrived home while she was out?

Mrs Jessop smiled again. "Come here," she said, and gave Alison's face a quick wipe. "Now then, if you want to go and meet him, run quickly. You'll catch him before he's home!"

But Alison felt worried. Two years was such a long time. She could just about remember her father. He was tall and ruddy-faced, and he wore sailor's clothes which smelled of tar and salt. He would not have changed very much in two years.

Alison was always being told how tall she had become, and how grown-up she was getting. Perhaps her father would not recognise the little girl he had left behind. Suddenly she remembered what she must do. "My pink bonnet!" she cried. "I must wear the pink bonnet, then he'll know it's me!" She ran inside the cottage, and hunted among all the coats and hats which were hanging on the back of the door. The little bonnet was on her wooden peg, a special one fixed low for her. She pulled off her woolly hat and placed the bonnet on her head.

"It's too small!" exclaimed Mrs Jessop.

"It can't be!" Alison was horrified. But her mother just laughed, and the bonnet did look very silly, perched on top of her head. It had a pink muslin frill around the front, and two thin ribbons hanging down on either side, which tied under the chin.

"It's too small," said Mrs Jessop again. "It's two years since you last wore it, and you've grown!"

"But I must wear it," said Alison, crushing the bonnet a bit further on to her head. "How will Pa know me unless I wear my pink bonnet?"

"He'll know you all right," said Mrs Jessop soothingly.

"But I promised I would wear it!" cried Alison, as she tried desperately to make the sides of the bonnet stretch a little.

"Oh, very well, if you must. I wondered why you were keeping the old thing." Smiling, her mother took the bonnet strings from Alison's impatient hands, and tied them under her chin.

As soon as it was done, Alison broke away, and raced off down the road to the docks. She was beginning to slow down, out of breath, when she saw in the distance two figures coming towards her along the road. She could see that they carried seamen's boxes on their shoulders. One of them stopped, and seemed to be looking at her.

"Pa!" she shouted, and ran faster than ever.

Enoch Jessop set down his heavy box when he saw the child running towards him. "That's her! That's her little pink bonnet!" he said to Jim Ashburn, the young man beside him. Then he stared at her and shook his head. "No

. . . it can't be . . ." he said.

"It's a pink bonnet all right," said Jim.

"Pa! Pa!" shouted Alison as she came into earshot.

She had completely forgotten that she was out of breath, and that her legs were beginning to feel tired. Her father held out his arms and she flew into them. He caught her up and swung her round in the air, just as he always used to.

"Well, well," he said, as he set her down again. He had not expected her to be quite so heavy. The bonnet had slipped back off her head now and lay on her shoulders. He looked at Alison, amazed at how much she had grown, and she looked up at him. His face was burnt brown from hot climates, and his sharp seaman's eyes had many wrinkles around them, from continually being narrowed against the wind and the strong light on the open sea.

"I've grown, Pa," she said. "The pink bonnet is too small!"

"I'm glad you wore it," said Mr Jessop, "for if you hadn't I wouldn't have known you."

"That's just what I said to Mammy!"

Mr Jessop chuckled. "I would have walked right by you," he said, winking at Jim beside him.

"No you wouldn't! I'd have shouted!" cried Alison.

The three of them laughed. Then Mr Jessop bent and swung his seaman's box on to his shoulders. He looked at his daughter and smiled. "Can't carry you on my shoulders any more, my little maid!"

"Indeed not! I'm nearly nine!" said Alison. Jim laughed at her. "Oh my, quite grown-up!" he said.

"Yes, Uncle Jim," replied Alison, ignoring the twinkle in his eye. Then her father took one of Alison's hands, and Jim took the other, and they set off home.

Back at the cottage, Mrs Jessop was preparing the tea. She bustled about in the one large room that took up most of the ground floor. The kettle was coming up to the boil on the iron hob next to the fire, and she set the teapot near it to warm. She went to the wooden dresser, and took down her best cups and saucers and plates, which had bright blue patterns on them. The plates were propped up in a neat row on the dresser so that the pictures on them could be seen. The cups were hanging from little hooks underneath. They were only taken down and used on special occasions. When she had laid the table, Mrs Jessop began to cut bread and butter. Her movements were quick and neat, and she hummed a cheerful little song to herself as she worked.

Suddenly the door burst open.

"Here's Pa!" shouted Alison. Mrs Jessop almost dropped the bread knife. She said nothing, but watched her husband as he stooped and came in through the low doorway.

"Home safely, lass," he said, and she went over to him.

"None too soon," she said, and they hugged each other.

Alison ran up as well, and tried to join in by hugging both of them at once. Her arms were much too short, so she tugged at her mother's skirts, and snuggled in between her parents instead. Jim Ashburn had waited in the cottage garden while all this was going on. Now he stepped shyly across the threshold.

"And you're right welcome too, Jim," said Mrs Jessop. "This home's yours too while you're ashore."

The greetings over, they all sat down to tea. West Country ham, Mrs Jessop's own scones, several different kinds of jam, thick clotted cream, and a rich, dark, fruit cake. Everything that Alison could wish for, and she ate until she was full to bursting.

Mr Jessop had little appetite, but seemed happy just to look around him at the familiar room. The mantelshelf over the fire was covered with strange objects from all over the world. An ivory elephant, a flute made from bamboo, an outlandish Eastern god carved from jade, and two great shining conch shells that the South Sea Islanders blow upon like horns. There were several snuff boxes, and some china mugs with pictures of famous seamen like Admiral Nelson on them. And there was Alison's collection too, of all the shells and other treasures she had found on the beach.

Mrs Jessop kept all these souvenirs carefully dusted, despite the fact that there were so many of them. Everything in the cottage was spotless, from the white lace curtains at the window to the stone flags of the floor.

After tea, when it began to get dark, and the firelight cast a warm, flickering glow over the room, Alison sat on a low stool at her father's feet. She showed him the big shell she had found on the beach, and he put it to his ear.

"That's a good one," he said. "You can hear the sea quite loudly."

"It's the best I've ever found," she said, and went to add it to her collection.

Mrs Jessop watched them quietly, while Jim began scraping and poking at the bowl of his pipe in preparation for lighting it.

"Nothing has changed," said Mr Jessop, gazing into the fire.

"Only me. I've grown!" said Alison. Then she asked, "What have you brought back for me this time?"

"Saucy girl! What have I brought back for you indeed!"

"Shhh, Alison!" said Mrs Jessop. "You look tired, Enoch."

"I am tired. The wind was against us all the way from Spain."

Jim looked up from his pipe. "Not quite all the way," he said.

"It seemed like it," said Mr Jessop.

"Mammy, can't I ask now?" said Alison. Her mother nodded. "Pa, what have you brought me?"

"Now, Allie, you shouldn't ask like that, it isn't very polite," interrupted her mother quickly, but Mr Jessop merely said: "She's but a child. Now, you go and lift the lid of my box, and see what you find."

Alison hurried over to her father's box and opened it. On the very top lay a little silver trumpet.

"Oh Pa! Look! Is it for me?" Jim and Mr Jessop burst out laughing.

"No, my maid, that's my call! My bosun's call." He held out his hand and Alison gave him the trumpet. Mr Jessop put it to his lips and blew. The sound it made was high and shrill like a whistle.

Jim grinned. "You'll have all the sailors in Plymouth standing to attention!" he said, and they laughed again.

"Can I have it, Pa?" asked Alison. Her mother was very shocked, but Mr Jessop promised that when his days at sea were over, and he had no more need of the bosun's call, he would give it to Alison. She said she would keep it for ever and ever when it became hers. She tried several times to blow the little trumpet, but no sound at all came out.

"I'll tell you what," said Mr Jessop, "you keep it while I'm home, and see if you can learn how to blow it."

"Oh Pa!"

"You mustn't lose it, Alison," warned her mother.

"She won't lose it. Now, Sal, what else is in my box?"

Mrs Jessop's face lit up. She was like a child herself as she went to help Alison. Together they lifted out a roll of material in bright foreign colours. Mrs Jessop ran it through her fingers.

"Silk! Oh Enoch – it's so fine. Much too good for such as we!" The silk was so delicate that her rough, work-worn hands were catching tiny threads as she stroked it, so she laid it on one side.

"Nothing is too good for you," said Mr Jessop. Then he gave a little shiver. "It's draughty, ain't it?" He put some more coal on the fire.

Alison rummaged deeper in the box. "Oh look, look! It's a fairy's stone!" She held up a beautiful piece of coral.

"That's right." Mr Jessop took out his pipe and lit it. He glanced over at the young man sitting on the other side of the fire. "Our Jim's going on his next voyage soon. He's taking off for the West Indies as a bosun."

"That's well done, Jim," said Mrs Jessop. Jim looked half-bashful and half-proud, and insisted that he owed everything to Mr Jessop, who had helped to keep him straight and steady on his earlier voyages. But the older man wasn't listening. He complained of the cold again, and Mrs Jessop brought his coat to wrap round him.

"I can't seem to get warm," he said. "I was too warm on board ship. I can't understand it." He sighed and drew his chair nearer to the fire.

Jim spoke again: "I'd like to ask you a favour, if you don't mind."

"Ask on, lad."

"Well, being steady on this last voyage, I've managed to put by a bit of money." He took a little tin box from his pocket. "I've got it in here," he said.

Alison came forward to have a look.

"It's pretty!" she cried. There was a design painted on the lid – a ring of roses and forget-me-nots, with a sailor and his girl in the centre. The box was fastened with a padlock.

"I've got nigh on fifty pounds here," went on Jim. "I wondered, like, if you'd keep the box for me. Till I get back from my next voyage. I have a fear I might get a bit wild without you behind me, Enoch."

"You won't, I'm sure of that."

"But I'd like to be on the safe side. Fifty pounds is a tidy bit to come back to."

"What d'you think, Sal? Would you mind taking care of Jim's box?" Mr Jessop asked.

"No, of course not," said Mrs Jessop. "I'll keep it safe."

"That's all right then, Jim," said Mr Jessop warmly, and there was a twinkle in his eye as he added: "A girl somewhere, is there?"

Jim cleared his throat. "One day, I hope," he said.

"Have you got the key safe?" Mrs Jessop asked, and he felt in his pocket and nodded.

Mr Jessop drew his chair even closer to the fire. Alison was now staring sleepily at the glowing coals, her head resting on the empty box.

"Did you have many storms this voyage, Pa?" she asked dreamily.

"No. Most of the time we needed wind," her father replied. "Except coming back from Spain. We could do with a bit more on the fire, Sal."

Mrs Jessop piled some more coals on the fire, as many as she could without blocking the chimney. Then she went to touch her husband's forehead. "That's very hot," she exclaimed.

But Mr Jessop was still shivering. "I seem to have a chill right in my bones," he said.

"When I have a chill Mammy puts me to bed," said Alison, blinking hard and trying to wake herself up.

"I think bed is the place for me," said Mr Jessop. He got up shakily, and gave Jim's tin box to his wife.

"May I look at it?" asked Alison. Her mother looked very disapproving, but Jim didn't mind, and she was allowed to take the box. She was so busy looking at the pictures, and tracing them with her finger, that she hardly noticed her father. He gave up the idea of going to bed, and returned to his warm chair by the fire. He was so unsteady that Jim went to help him across the room.

"Is it fever?" he asked. Mrs Jessop shrugged her shoulders and frowned anxiously. She went over to the wooden settle that stood against the wall, and pulled out the low truckle bed that was stored there out of sight during the daytime. She moved it close to the fire, and began to prepare it for her husband, glancing at him with a worried expression from time to time.

Mr Jessop was very ill, and stayed in the truckle bed close to the fire for several days.

Jim stayed with the family for a while and did what he could for Mrs Jessop. But his ship was due to leave Plymouth, and very soon he had to go and join it.

"We shall miss you," said Mrs Jessop. "But we'll keep your box safe, don't worry."

Jim went over to the bed, but Mr Jessop was asleep.

"I hope all will be well," he said, and went on his way with his seaman's box on his back.

Mr Jessop did not seem to improve after his friend's departure. Any loud noise or disturbance upset him, and Alison found it hard to keep still and quiet all the time, so Mrs Jessop sent her outside whenever she could.

Alison was happy wandering about on the beach. She took her bucket for collecting shells, and the bosun's call was always in her pocket.

It was a few days before she managed to get a note out of it, and when she did it happened quite suddenly, without her expecting it. She was down on the sands one morning, and when she blew, the shrill, clear note sounded. A seaman nearby was very startled. He stopped in his tracks and looked all around him. When he saw that it was Alison who had blown the bosun's call he grinned and waved at her. Alison hardly noticed him. She ran back to the cottage full of excitement, and rushed in, leaving the door wide open, and letting in a blast of cold air.

Mrs Jessop was giving her husband a drink of water.

His eyes were bright, and his face very flushed. He kept trying to throw off the covers. Mrs Jessop patiently put them back each time.

"Pa! Pa! I can blow the trumpet!"

Mrs Jessop had gone to shut the door, and she wasn't quick enough to stop Alison. She blew the bosun's call loudly. Mr Jessop sat up, his eyes glowing.

"Weighing the anchor? Are we at sea?"

"You're at home, Enoch," said his wife, taking Alison by the arm.

Mr Jessop seemed puzzled. "I heard . . ."

"No one," soothed his wife.

Alison tried to interrupt, but her mother signalled her to be quiet.

"Let the little maid come near," said Mr Jessop, suddenly aware that she was there. She crept up, and sat on the bed. He took her hand and spoke quietly to her. "I'm a-riding into harbour, my lass, sailing into a quiet haven."

"Hush, dear, try to sleep," said Mrs Jessop, but her husband went on: "Have you got that box of Jim's safe, Sal? Jim's little box?"

"It's safe in the cupboard, Pa," said Alison, leaning across. Her father's voice was very quiet and weak, and she could hardly hear him.

"Keep it as you value your life," he whispered. "It's Jim's guarantee he means to go steady."

"I'll guard it, Enoch," said Mrs Jessop. She spoke quietly, trying to keep back her tears.

Alison had not realised that anything was wrong. She leaned across again. "Pa, I can blow the trumpet," she said proudly.

Her father opened his eyes. He seemed to be amused. "Is that the last trumpet, my little maid?" he said.

Mrs Jessop put her hands over her face.

"Will you blow it clear for me, my pretty," Mr Jessop

whispered. Alison blew the bosun's call loud and clear. Mr Jessop smiled. Then he went very still. Alison could hear her mother crying. She looked at her father. His eyes were open, but he was not looking at her. His gaze was fixed.

"Pa! Pa!" she shrieked. He did not stir or reply. He could not see her. Alison was afraid, and ran out of the room. She ran down to the edge of the sea, and shrieked and shouted to the waves: "Pa! Pa!" There was no answer but the surge of the sea and the cry of the gulls: "Kaa! Kaa!"

Chapter Two

"Why can't we go on the train, Mammy?" asked Alison. Everything had been cleared away, and they were standing in the middle of the front room, surrounded by boxes and bundles. It was a couple of weeks later. Since her father's death the little cottage had been full of people. Relatives she hardly knew, all swathed in black, had picked her up and cried over her. Now at last she and her mother were alone again.

"We can't go by train. It isn't to be thought of." Mrs Jessop frowned and looked at the purse in her hand.

"But we've got the money!"

"Alison! That's to feed us until I find some work to do." Mrs Jessop closed her fingers tightly round the purse. The tin box with the sailor and his girl on the lid was on the bare wooden table. She picked it up, shook it, and then took a big knife from one of the bundles and tried to break the padlock and force open the lid.

"That's Uncle Jim's box!" said Alison. Mrs Jessop looked at her for a moment, then put down the knife and gave her the box. Alison put it carefully inside the big seaman's chest which had belonged to her father. She laid it next to the pink bonnet which rested on top of all her other souvenirs. Everything was gone from the mantelshelf except a big piece of seaweed, which she had hung there to tell the weather by. She went to take it down.

"Don't be silly, Alison. You can't take that!"

"But we'll need it!"

"It'll be no use to us in London. How can it tell the weather in dirty old London?"

"Is it dirty there?" asked Alison.

"Dirty and dark and dismal," replied her mother.

"Why do we have to go there then?"

Mrs Jessop sighed. "I might find some work there."

Alison took down the seaweed and put it in a bag. Then she placed it in the trunk and shut the lid. "Will we come back?" she asked.

"Perhaps," said her mother.

"*I* shall come back," said Alison, and went to the door, to look down over the beach to the waves and the wild sky.

It was a very different view that Alison looked at a year later from the window of their new home in London. Mrs Jessop had rented a little room on the top floor of an old building called Adler's Court. Opposite were the grimy walls of another tenement building, and down below in the courtyard children were playing around a litter of rubbish. Adler's Court had certainly seen better days.

Alison sighed and turned away. There always seemed to be a smell of stale cooking lingering about, and the few bits of furniture were covered in a thin film of gritty dust. Everything had to be dusted every day. Alison took a duster and went to the mantelshelf. Her shells were there, and the seaweed. In the middle was the silver trumpet, and underneath, next to the drying washing, hung the pink bonnet.

Everything had changed, except for these few familiar objects. Even Alison herself was paler and taller.

A shrill whistle came from below. Alison ran to the window and looked down. The children were still scrambling about on the rubbish, but it was not one of them who had whistled. She could just see an older boy of about thirteen looking up at her. He was laden with a heavy bundle of washing, and in one hand he was balancing a covered plate. Alison took down the bosun's call and blew a loud clear note which echoed round the courtyard. The boy grinned at her and went into the house.

As he opened the door a great cloud of steam billowed

out. His mother was a washerwoman, and the kitchen was usually full of steam.

"Get out from under me feet, you nuisance! GET OUT! OUT!" a woman's voice shouted harshly. Alison thought her friend was being scolded, and craned her neck anxiously to see what was going on.

A large, rough-looking man stumbled out of the kitchen, muttering to himself. "Can't even sit in me own house," he grumbled. He leaned against the wall for a moment, then kicked out at a small girl who was sitting on the doorstep. She dodged out of his way, and he slumped down on the step in her place. Alison went back to her dusting, relieved that it was not her friend Johnnie who was in trouble this time.

He, meanwhile, was heaving the big bag of washing through the kitchen, pushing through a crowd of his small brothers and sisters, who were dabbling in the puddles on the floor and blowing bubbles with an old clay pipe.

"Got some more dirties for you, Mam!" he shouted.

His mother, Mrs Cleaver, was a big strong woman. Her bare red arms were up to the elbows in the wash tub, and she merely glanced at him and jerked her head towards a corner of the crowded room.

"Put 'em there, Johnnie," she said. "And there's a pile of mangling for you to do over there."

Johnnie looked at the great heap of wet clothes beside the tall iron mangle.

"I've got Alison's dinner 'ere, Mam. I'll just run up with it 'afore it gets cold." He headed for the stairs with the plate.

"Don't you stay playing up there!" shouted Mrs Cleaver after him. Johnnie ran full speed up the stairs and whistled outside Alison's door. "I've brought you a slice of pudding, Allie!" he called. She let him in. "It was all I could get with one penny." He gave her the plate.

Alison lifted off the paper cover and breathed in the fragrant smell of the pudding. "I'm so hungry!" she said.

"Then you should have given me some more money," said Johnnie. "Don't your Mammy give you enough for a proper dinner?"

Alison tucked into the slice of pudding. "Yes, but I'm saving it."

"What for?"

"A petticoat."

Johnnie stared at Alison. "You got a petticoat," he said. He could see the hem of it peeping from under the edge of her skirt.

Alison was still gulping down the pudding. She paused to explain. "But Mammy hasn't. She needs a nice one." The last of the pudding disappeared. Alison sighed with satisfaction. "Mmm! I'm glad you're my friend, bringing me my dinner. We didn't have to buy dinner when we lived by the sea."

Johnnie snorted. "You have to buy everything!"

"But Mammy used to cook the dinner herself, then."

"She must've bought the things to cook."

"She grew them!" said Alison.

Johnnie was not at all convinced. "How do dinners grow?"

"Well, cabbages grow, and potatoes, and beans. They grow in the garden."

"Beans? What's beans?" asked Johnnie.

"Long green things," explained Alison, wiping her plate clean. "There's a nice warm petticoat in the pawn shop. It costs nine pennies. Mammy's seen it." She got out her handkerchief, which had some money tied into the corner. She shook it out on to the table.

Johnnie's eyes widened. "That's a sight of pennies!" he said.

"Eight, nine, ten . . ." Alison counted them. "Will you

come with me to buy it?"

"Can't," said Johnnie quickly.

"But I can't go alone! I've never bought anything on my own before! And London is so big. I thought you were my friend!"

"There's the mangling to do. Then I got to take the clean things back."

"What about after that?"

"Can't truly say." Johnnie was edging towards the door.

"But you're my friend!" cried Alison. Johnnie looked out of the window and whistled a little tune to himself. "I thought friends helped," said Alison sadly. Then she cheered up as an idea struck her. "Can I come with you when you take the clean things? We could buy the petticoat on the way back."

"You'd have to walk fast."

"I will."

"And if you come, will you tell me some more about your Pa? And the sea?"

"Of course!" said Alison. Johnnie had never been out of London, and Alison's tales of her old life in the little cottage by the beach fascinated him.

"Johnnie! Come on down 'ere!" A loud shout echoed up the stairs.

"There she goes!" Johnnie grinned and slipped out of the room.

Later on that afternoon Alison hurried after him as he carried the heavy parcel of clean washing out of the dismal courtyard and through the crowded streets. People pushed and shoved them, and carts rattled and rumbled over the cobblestones. The iron-bound cartwheels and the great iron shoes of the huge horses made such a noise that it was impossible to hear themselves speak, except when there was a traffic jam, which happened very often in the narrower streets. Alison kept close to Johnnie, and held on to his coat when the crowds were particularly bad. Then she waited while he slipped down the area steps of a big house and delivered the washing at the kitchen door. He pocketed the money for his mother, and then they ran together to the little back street where the pawn shop was.

"That's the one!" panted Alison, pointing to some petticoats hanging up in the grimy window. "That's the kind Mammy likes!"

They went into the dark, musty-smelling shop, stepping over the heaps of clothing and boxes of dusty china which littered the floor. A pale young man who looked as if he had never been out in the fresh air all his life lifted down the petticoats with a long wooden pole and tossed them on the counter for Alison to look at. She turned them over.

"This woollen drab one," she said. "It's so soft and warm. And it's all wool. I don't think there's a bit of cotton in it." She paid for it, and they set off home.

Once they were back in the little room, and Alison had mended the fire, Johnnie was impatient for a story. "What about your Pa, then?" he said.

"Oh, he was lovely! All salty like the sea."

"Salty?" Johnnie frowned. "Like what you eat, you mean?"

"Sort of."

"Tell me about his ship."

"I've told you that."

"Tell me again!" said Johnnie impatiently.

"It had great big sails to catch the wind, and clean white boards on the deck . . ."

Johnnie's eyes were shining already as a picture began to take shape in his mind. "All scrubbed by your Pa . . . " he said.

"No, no! Pa didn't scrub the decks! He blew the trumpet. I've told you!"

Johnnie thought for a moment. "If I go to sea on a ship, will you give me the trumpet?"

"You don't need it. You can whistle loud enough yourself," said Alison. Johnnie went to the mantelshelf and looked at the trumpet.

"I hope you don't go to sea," said Alison. "You might catch the fever like Pa."

"I never catch nothing," said Johnnie. "We had two babies died of the fever, but I never got it. Can I listen to the sea?" Alison nodded. He took down her special big shell and put it to his ear. He shut his eyes and smiled.

"That could be the Indian Ocean," said Alison.

"One day I'll go there and I'll bring you back a shell even better than this," said Johnnie, dreamily.

Downstairs in the kitchen, Mrs Jessop was passing through with a basket of food on her arm.

"Afternoon, Mrs Cleaver," she said. Johnnie's mother looked up from her washing and wiped her forehead with the back of her hand.

"Tell that son of mine he's wanted down here," she said.

"I will," said Mrs Jessop.

The small ragged girl who had been sitting on the step earlier was now in the corner rocking a cradle. She watched Mrs Jessop intently, and crept quietly up to see what was in the food basket.

"Oh, Mrs Jessop, I almost forgot!" Mrs Cleaver fished in the front of her blouse with wet hands, and pulled out a crumpled envelope. "A sailor lad brought this for you." She held out the letter.

"Thank you!" said Mrs Jessop, peering shortsightedly at the letter. As she made her way upstairs, the small girl tip-toed after her, with a quick glance to make sure her mother wasn't looking.

Alison was laying out her shell collection on the table.

"This one's from Australia," she said.

"Where's that?" asked Johnnie.

"Underneath us," said Alison.

Johnnie looked despairingly at her. "What?" he said. Footsteps sounded on the stairs.

"Mammy!" said Alison. She quickly hid the petticoat. "A surprise!" she whispered to Johnnie, and ran to hug Mrs Jessop as she came in.

"Your mother wants you, Johnnie," said Mrs Jessop.

"Here we go again," sighed Johnnie, and loped off downstairs, two at a time.

"Come on in, Bess," said Mrs Jessop to the small girl who was hiding outside on the landing. "Shut the door, and come on in. Now, shall we have some supper?"

Bess peered into the basket. "You got eggs!" she said. "I likes eggs."

"Then you shall have one," said Mrs Jessop, as she got out the knives and forks.

"A *whole* egg?" Bess's eyes were wide.

"And bread with it too," said Alison. "But Mammy, there's only two eggs, and Bess makes three."

"I had a big dinner at the house today, so I don't need one," said Mrs Jessop. "The cook has some more work for me, so I shall go back again tomorrow. We'll be all right for money for another few days."

She began to boil water for the eggs, filling a little pan and setting it on the fire. Alison sliced and buttered the bread. Bess was yawning and stretching. She groaned and rubbed her back.

"Does your back hurt you?" asked Mrs Jessop.

"Don't it just!" replied Bess, making a face. "It's lugging that big baby about. I been lugging babies ever since I was a baby. There's a new one every year." Mrs Jessop left the fireside and went to rub the little girl's back. Bess watched Alison greedily.

"You got butter, too!" she said, licking her lips. Then she said loudly, "I hate babies. They're heavy and they stink!"

"Oh dearie, dearie me!" exclaimed Mrs Jessop, but she was not really cross. She gave Bess a little pat on the head. "Now come and wash your hands, Bess my girl."

"What for?"

"Because you're just about to have your food, and your hands are very dirty!"

"That stinking baby done it," said Bess, looking at her hands.

A few moments later she was sitting up at the table and scraping round and round the inside of her empty egg-shell.

"That were a good egg," she said. "Not very stale." Mrs Jessop handed her the last piece of bread and butter, which she wolfed down in a few mouthfuls.

Alison was still hungry, but she only said, watching Bess spilling crumbs all down her front and all over the floor, "You don't let *me* eat like that!"

"You're different, Allie," said her mother.

Bess yawned and stretched again, groaning as she felt her aching back.

"Have a little lie down, lovey," suggested Mrs Jessop, and took her over to the bed, where she covered her with a shawl and gave her a quick kiss.

"Oh my," sighed Bess, and closed her eyes. Mrs Jessop started to clear the tea things away.

"The letter, Mammy!" said Alison. Her mother cleared a space on the table, fetched the letter, and they spread it out in the pool of candle-light.

"Shall I read it, Mam?" said Alison impatiently as Mrs Jessop searched for her glasses. She took it and read aloud:

"Dear Sal, I am sad to hear my old friend Enoch has passed over. This is to tell you that I am in Plymouth now and shall come to you in London for my box, as I needs the money. Hoping this will find you as it leaves me, Yours, Jim Ashburn."

"It's Uncle Jim! Will he find us, do you think?"

"If his letter found us, then he will too," said Mrs Jessop. She was very pleased, and went to look for Jim's tin box at once. Very gently, so as not to wake Bess, she pulled her husband's big sea chest from under the bed and dragged it into the light. She peered into it and felt around inside.

"Have you been messing in here, Alison?"

"No, I never touch it, Mammy."

Mrs Jessop had gone very pale. "The tin box has gone," she said.

The note of panic in her voice woke up Bess from her doze, and she began listening from the shadowy corner where she lay on the bed.

"Where could it have gone?" Alison cried as she rummaged in the box.

"You sure you never shown that tin box to no one?" Mrs Jessop gave Alison a shake. "Are you quite sure?"

"Never!" said Alison. Mrs Jessop heaved the box over on its side and tipped everything on to the floor. She searched frantically through all the oddments, muttering to herself: "I guarded it all these months. Oh dearie, dearie me! How can I tell Jim?" Alison watched her in silence now, feeling rather frightened, and Bess from her dark corner was watching too, though she kept very still.

Alison crouched where she was on the floor for a long time, not sure what to do next. Mrs Jessop sat with her handkerchief over her mouth and muttered to herself from time to time: "Oh dearie me, what are we going to do?" she leaned her head in her hands. "How can I face him?"

"It's not your fault, Mammy." Alison began to tidy the scattered things back into the box.

"I've let his money be lost!" cried Mrs Jessop. "I promised your father I would keep it safe, and I've let it be lost!"

"Was there a lot of money in the tin box?"

"All his savings. Fifty pounds!"

Neither of them noticed Bess, who was now wide awake, and listening to their conversation with great interest.

"And there's no money to pay it back," sighed Mrs Jessop.

"There's that!" Alison pointed to her mother's purse. "And I've got a penny." She got her one remaining penny out. Mrs Jessop did not notice.

"Where can I find such a large sum?" she said to herself.

"Mam . . ." said Alison after a pause. There was no reply. "Mam! I've got a surprise for you." She pulled out the petticoat from its hiding place. Mrs Jessop did not see. "Mammy! Look! It's a surprise for you." She held out the woollen petticoat and pushed it into her mother's hands.

"A surprise?" Mrs Jessop ran her fingers slowly over the material. "Alison – where did you get this?"

"I bought it."

"What with? You haven't any money."

"I saved it from my dinner money."

Mrs Jessop stared at her, then her eyes swam with tears, and she gave Alison a tight hug. "Oh my lovely! Oh, dearie me . . . I thought for a moment . . . Oh dear, there now!" She fumbled for her handkerchief and blew her nose. "That's better. Such a nice, warm petticoat! Just what I wanted." She stood up and held it against herself. It was a little short, but she lifted up the hem and found there was a big tuck in it.

"Look, I can let it down nicely. You know a good thing when you see one, Allie. I expect it belonged to a decent body in its day. I shall wear it tomorrow. Now come along Allie, it's well past your bedtime."

"What about Bess?" Bess was stretched out on the little bed with her eyes tightly shut.

"She's fast asleep, poor mite," Mrs Jessop smiled. "Shall we let her have a night away from the baby?"

"But what about you, Mammy?" The bed was just about big enough for Alison and her mother, but there certainly was not room for three.

"I'll sleep on the big chair for tonight."

So Alison lay down beside Bess on the bed, and after all the excitement and the worry of the day, she was asleep in a very few moments.

Chapter Three

Mrs Jessop did not sleep at all that night. She scarcely even sat down on the big chair. She kept getting up and pacing up and down the room, sometimes peering out of the window at the dark sky, and sometimes looking at Alison and Bess where they lay peacefully sleeping.

When the patch of sky at the window began to get lighter, she put on her new petticoat, and then gently shook Alison. "Look, Allie," she whispered, "it fits perfect round the waist."

Alison yawned and sat up. "It'll keep you warm, won't it?" she said, pulling the blankets up around her as she shivered in the cold morning air.

Mrs Jessop fetched Alison's old woollen jacket and put it round her. "You need a new jacket," she said. "This one is all darns and much too tight." She put on her hat ready to go out. "There's still some bread and butter for your breakfast."

"Did I hear bread and butter?" Bess sat up in bed, instantly awake.

"You shall have some, Bess," said Mrs Jessop, then she spoke quietly to Alison. "I must go now. If Uncle Jim comes before I'm back, make him some tea, and say nothing about you know what. Goodbye, my chicks!" She gave Alison and Bess a quick kiss.

"You two do a lot of kissing," said Bess, as Mrs Jessop went out. "Now, what about that bread and butter?" She jumped out of bed and waited impatiently while Alison laid the breakfast table and set everything out in its proper place. Then there was a happy silence as she tackled her first slice.

Alison decided to set her a good example. "Would you like some more bread and butter, Bess?" she asked, passing the plate in her best manner. Bess snatched another slice and gobbled it down without a word of thanks.

"Oh, listen to that horrible thing!" she said, as the baby's shrill cry drifted up the stairs. She stretched luxuriously. "Well, I'm much obliged to your Ma for letting me sleep here without that baby hanging round me neck. I wish I could be here all the time."

"Oh, no – you couldn't do that!" said Alison quickly. "Mammy can't sleep in the chair every night."

"She didn't sleep in it last night." Bess told Alison how her mother had spent the night pacing up and down and muttering to herself. "And I don't blame her with all that there money stole!" she added.

"You were listening!" cried Alison.

"I heard a few bits, like. About all that gold in a tin box, and that sailor bloke what's coming back here for it. He'll have your Ma put in jail!"

"You wicked girl!"

"Well *I* didn't steal it." Bess pushed her chair back and got up. "I reckon it's a lame story 'bout it being lost. I could 'a' thought up a better one'n that myself . . ."

"Go back home!" shouted Alison. "I don't like you any more! I think you're dirty and mean!"

"All right, all right – mind your manners," said Bess, imitating Alison and sticking out her tongue.

"*Bess!* Come down 'ere to this baby, you little demon!" yelled Mrs Cleaver up the stairs as the baby's howls grew louder.

"And don't come back here again, you nasty thing!" shouted Alison, banging the door shut after her and leaning against it.

It was still quite dark as Mrs Jessop walked through the streets to the big house where she worked. Everyone else seemed to be hurrying to get to their work as well. The pavements were packed with people pushing and jostling each other. Suddenly, above all the bustle and rush, a bright clear whistle like a bird call sounded. Mrs Jessop stopped to listen. For a moment she thought she had heard a nightingale, as she used to sometimes in Devon. Then she saw Johnnie standing on the corner by the pawn shop with a pile of dirty washing at his feet. As the people passed him, one or two stopped and gave him a coin.

"Johnnie!" said Mrs Jessop, very shocked. "What's this?"

"I'm not a-begging, Mrs Jessop," called Johnnie cheerfully when he saw her. "I'm giving people a bit of cheer on their way to work, and they're giving me a bit of payment!"

"Oh, I see." Mrs Jessop could not help smiling.

"I needs to get some money by me," said Johnnie, confiding in her. "I means to be a sailor, and I must buy a little silver trumpet like Alison's Pa had . . ."

"I reckon you won't need one!" laughed Mrs Jessop. "You *are* one! But here's a ha'penny towards it, for it's a cheering thing to hear you." She gave him a coin and moved on. As Mrs Jessop walked past, she saw in the window of the pawn shop a little woollen jacket, grey with a red border. It was just Alison's size. She sighed and tried not to look at it as she hurried on.

But the little jacket stayed at the back of her mind all day, as she scrubbed and washed up at the big house. She worked mostly in the scullery, next to the big kitchen. Sounds of chopping and peeling and all sorts of delicious smells filtered through to her as she wrung out a pile of clean dishcloths. The cook kept bustling in on her with floury hands.

"I ain't got so much for you to do today, Mrs J.," she said. "You can wash down the floor out there when I'm finished, but I can't be doing with you just now. I'm in the middle of me meat pies. 'Ave a sit down dear, for five minutes. You looks like you could do with it."

"Thank you," said Mrs Jessop. She spread the dish-cloths out to dry, and then sat down in the scullery on a small wooden chair, but she found it hard to sit idle for long. In her basket was a little pair of scissors and her spectacles. She got them out, then hid behind the scullery door for a moment to take off the petticoat. Then she sat down again and began to unpick the hem.

It was very firmly sewn with tiny stitches, and it took her a long time to unpick. Suddenly she felt something thick in the material of the tuck. She squeezed and poked at it, then unpicked a little further, and pulled out a folded piece of paper. She smoothed it out. It was a banknote! She gasped and jumped to her feet. The scissors fell out of her lap, and as she stooped to pick them up her spectacles fell off her nose and broke on the stone floor.

"Oh dearie me," she said, fumbling blindly for them. "Now that be tragic!" She picked them up. The lenses were completely shattered. She put them away, and peered at the banknote again.

"Looks like a five to me . . ." she muttered. "Five pounds it must be. Five pounds!" She sat down abruptly and took a deep breath.

"Mrs Jessop!" called the cook from the kitchen. Mrs Jessop slid the note into her purse and went to answer.

Bess stayed in the kitchen at home all day, minding the baby. Every time it whimpered she rocked the cradle vigorously until it was quiet again. In the afternoon her mother and Johnnie went out with a load of clean washing to deliver, and she was left alone with her father. He slouched by the fire on a broken chair, half asleep. His eyelids drooped and his face was very red. He belched quietly to himself, then coughed and woke up to aim a

large gob of spit into the fire. Bess watched him with her bright, hard little eyes.

"And what are you a-staring at?" he demanded crossly. "Take your eyes off of me!"

"I'm wondering when our Johnnie's going to start drinking," she said cheekily.

"Eh?" he grunted.

"They all does it all the time," she continued, rocking the cradle.

"You bit of impudence! What d'you mean?"

"I'm glad I was born a girl. Men are worth nothing."

Mr Cleaver growled angrily and coughed again. "I'll tan your hide till it smokes," he warned.

Bess looked at him thoughtfully. "All men drinks and has wives as supports them," she said, unperturbed by his threats. "And they all beats their children. Seems men ain't got no sort of use at all . . ."

Cleaver grabbed a handy three-legged stool and flung it at Bess. She ducked, and as the stool hit the wall, one of the legs fell off. The baby began to roar.

"Now see what you done!" said Cleaver, wincing at the noise. Bess shoved the cradle with her foot and set it rocking again. Her father sank back in his chair once more and the kitchen fell quiet again.

"Father . . ." said Bess, after a long pause.

"Shut up! I want no more of your sauce."

"Wouldn't you like to hear . . ."

"*Shut up!*"

"It's a good tale what I heard upstairs last night." Cleaver shifted in his chair and yawned. "Them goodie-goodies upstairs have really done it now . . ." continued Bess.

"What you on about?" Cleaver was not very fond of the Jessops, and Bess knew it.

"They been thieving!" she whispered.

"Come on! That Mrs Jessop ain't a thief, surely. What's the story?"

"She was left a box of gold to take care of . . ."

"Gold?" Cleaver leaned forward in his chair. A flicker of interest showed in his red-rimmed eyes. "And she 'ave stole it?" he asked.

Bess nodded. "She was keeping it for a sailor man," she said. Cleaver gave a thoughtful grunt and began to poke the fire in a meditative way. "Will he have her put away?" asked Bess.

"She deserves it, don't she?"

"And how will she enjoy that?" wondered Bess. Her eyes glinted maliciously. Her father grinned across at her, and for a moment they looked very alike, side by side in the firelight. Then Bess began to laugh, a wicked, hysterical laugh. Her father clouted her on the side of the head.

"Stop that, you little witch, or I'll knock your head right off!"

He went back to glowering at the fire, and Bess slyly stuck out her tongue at him. Then the baby began to cry once more, and Bess had to take him from the cradle and walk around the room with him. Conversation was at an end for the time being.

Chapter Four

Alison had polished the old tin teapot until she could see her face in it. She held it up to look at herself, gave it a final rub and put it on the table, together with the best blue and white china that had come from the cottage. She poked the fire, and was just about to put the kettle on the hob when there was a heavy step on the stair, and a loud knock on the door. Alison picked up the poker, thinking it was one of the Cleavers.

"Go away!" she shouted. The door opened.

"Is this Mrs Jessop's room, little girl?" asked a tall sun-burnt young man, peering round the door.

"Uncle Jim!" cried Alison.

"Alison?" Jim stared at her for a moment in disbelief, before coming in and taking his hat off. He looked around at the dingy little room with its few bits of battered furniture.

"Looks like you've had a bit of a shipwreck, gal," he said at last. "You're living here like a couple of castaways. I guess your Pa dying . . ." He stopped himself and went on again after a moment. "What I mean to say is, well, when I was on the sea I kept thinking back to you in that pretty cottage with all your things around you. This room, it ain't the place for you and your Mammy."

"Beggars can't be choosers," said Alison.

"Well, yes . . ." Jim scratched his head thoughtfully, and smiled at Alison. "I'll tell you what, my lovely, I got a bit put by from this voyage, and when I open that little tin box you've been keeping for me I'll have a bit more, so maybe I can give you a helping hand, eh?"

Alison did not dare look at him. She took the poker and turned away to poke the fire so that he could not see her red face.

"You miss your Pa, eh?" he said, seeing that she was upset.

"Very much," said Alison and added quickly, "would you like a drink of tea, Uncle Jim?"

"Wouldn't I just!" he said, sitting down by the fire and stretching out his long legs. "Yes, I got a nice tidy little bit in that box, Allie – a nice little bit tucked away." He chuckled happily to himself and got his pipe and tobacco out. "Mind if I have a smoke?" he asked. She shook her head.

"Where's your Mammy?"

"Out charring, Uncle Jim."

"Charring?" Jim lowered the pipe he was filling. "Hey, hey, poor soul! And her such a proud little body. Poor soul!" He lit his pipe and puffed at it for a few minutes, frowning. "Have you had your tea yet, my flower?" he asked.

"Mammy brings my supper," said Alison.

"But you could do with a spot of tea! Put some colour back into those pale cheeks! Come on, we'll take a stroll and buy a bit to eat. Get your bonnet." He nodded towards the old pink bonnet hanging by the mantelshelf.

"It don't fit no more," said Alison.

"Well, that's to be expected, I suppose!" Jim laughed. "Come along, make yourself ship-shape." Alison put on her coat and hat and they went out.

On her way home from work that evening, Mrs Jessop called in at the pawn shop. Johnnie was there on the corner again, whistling to the passers-by. "You looking for another petticoat?" he called. "Ain't you suited with the one you've got?"

"I'm very well suited," she replied, "but I've had a little windfall of money, and I thought I'd get Alison a jacket." She showed Johnnie the grey jacket with the red border which was hanging in the window.

"She'll like that. Keep her warm and cheer us up to look at her!" said Johnnie. Mrs Jessop laughed and went into the shop.

The same pale young man who had served Alison was sitting behind the counter with his feet up, looking very bored. "Yes?" he said, rather rudely.

"I want to buy a little knitted jacket."

"How little?"

"Well it's for my daughter . . ."

"She might be six foot for all I know." The young man yawned at Mrs Jessop. She showed him how tall Alison was, and he slowly got to his feet and tossed a few old jerseys on to the counter.

"There you are then," he said, and sat down again.

Mrs Jessop turned over a few of the jerseys, but they were very old and worn, and some of them were not very clean.

"There's one in the window . . ." she began.

"The winder?" said the young man as if he had no idea what she meant.

"Yes. A little grey one with a red border."

"Ah. That's for show." The young man sank back in his chair.

"Well that's the one I want!" said Mrs Jessop firmly. She was beginning to get a bit tired of this young man.

"You would, wouldn't you," he complained, and slouched over to the window to unhook the jacket.

"That'll be half-a-crown," he said, throwing it on to the counter.

"It was marked one and threepence!"

"It's gone up," said the young man, giving Mrs Jessop a nasty look.

"It's one and threepence! Look, there's the ticket!" said Johnnie, suddenly appearing from behind Mrs. Jessop. He pointed to a small piece of paper the young man had just pulled off the jacket.

"All right, all right, have it your own way," the young man said, looking crestfallen. His face fell even more when Mrs Jessop asked to see some socks.

"Socks?" he said. "You got me on a right merry-go-round, ain't you?"

"That comes to one and sixpence, I think," said Mrs Jessop, when she had chosen a pair of socks.

"Just about," said the young man, hoping to be rid of her as soon as possible. Mrs Jessop got out the banknote she had found in the hem of the petticoat. Johnnie's mouth fell open with surprise. So did the young man's.

"Ain't you got no smaller?" he asked.

"No." The young man suddenly became very wide-awake. He pursed up his lips into a thin line and, with an odd look at Mrs Jessop, disappeared into the back room of the shop. He stayed for a long time, and when he came out again, he did not bring her change as she was expecting, but told her to wait, and served another woman who had come into the shop. Mrs Jessop waited.

"What about my bit of change, sir?" she said after a while.

"Bit of change indeed! We can't give *that* amount of change in a hurry!"

Mrs Jessop waited and waited. It began to get dark. Once Johnnie stuck his head round the door, and said: "You still here?" The young man served several other customers and lit a lamp on the counter. He kept disappearing into the back of the shop.

Finally a short fat man with a bald head and a greasy waistcoat came out. "My name's Hynes," he said. "I'm the manager. Will you come with me?" Mrs Jessop followed him into the back of the shop. He took her to the office, a musty-smelling, dark little room.

"Is this the woman?" said a tall policeman who was standing by the wall. Mrs Jessop nearly jumped out of her skin.

"It is," said Mr Hynes, sitting behind his desk.

"Sir, can I have my change and go home?" asked Mrs Jessop, seeing her banknote lying on the desk. "My little girl is all alone . . ."

The policeman coughed. He picked up the note. "Exactly how much change are you expecting from this note?" he asked. Mrs Jessop became very flustered and went red in the face as she tried to work out the sum.

"Well," she began, "the jacket and socks are one and sixpence, and the change must be the balance between that and five pounds."

"Madam, don't make fools of the law. Where did you get this note?" said the policeman.

"Well, sir, I found it in the hem of a petticoat."

"A petticoat?" the policeman frowned.

"It was bought here."

"Here?" Mr Hynes got up and leaned over the desk, staring hard at Mrs Jessop.

"My little girl bought it. Is it not a five pound note, sir? I don't see too well . . ." Mrs Jessop's legs were trembling.

"Don't see too well, eh?" Mr Hynes began to laugh, and even the policeman permitted himself a brief smile. Then he said sternly: "This note is for fifty pounds, and I want to know the truth. How did it come into your possession?"

Mrs Jessop was so shocked she could barely stand up and all she could say was: "Oh sir . . . Oh dearie me . . ."

Chapter Five

Alison and Jim Ashburn were just back from their shopping trip. Jim was unwrapping the food they had bought while Alison made the tea.

"Oh my eyes! That's a spread ain't it!" said a shrill voice. Bess had crept up the stairs after them, following the smell of mutton pies, and when she saw all the food spread out on the table she just could not keep quiet.

"Go away Bess, I'm busy just now," said Alison.

Bess looked greedily at the mutton pies, the sweet pastries and the big crusty loaf of bread. "You ain't a-going to eat all that yourselves!" she said.

Jim looked at her thin pale face with its roughly cropped fringe. "I think we could spare a bit for you my dear," he said.

Bess sidled into the room. "I loves mutton pies more than anything," she said. She looked at Jim with her bright eyes. Alison wished she would go away, but she did not dare say anything, so she got on with making the tea.

"My word, you're a hungry little maid!" said Jim, as Bess demolished a large mutton pie.

"Everyone's hungry here," said Alison, putting the teapot on the table and sitting down. When the tea was poured, Bess grabbed a cup and drank noisily. All the time her eyes were fixed on Jim.

"Be you the sailor chap what left the box with the gold in it?" Jim set his mug down with a bump.

"Who told you about my box?" he asked abruptly.

"She was listening to Mammy and me . . ." Alison tried to explain.

"I heard . . ." Bess's eyes glinted.

"Go back to your baby!" said Alison, trying to stop what she knew was coming.

"I *heard* as the box is stolen, Mr Sailor Man!"

"What?" said Jim.

"Go home, Bess!" cried Alison desperately.

"Stole, did she say?" asked Jim, very perplexed. The room went quiet. Bess got up and edged towards the door.

"Stole! They's thieves here!" and she ran out.

Alison burst into tears. "We didn't take the gold, we didn't!"

"Is the box gone, then?"

Alison nodded. "Mammy's heart is nearly broke!"

"Now then, dry your eyes," said Jim kindly, for Alison could hardly speak for crying. "When was it stolen?"

Alison blew her nose on his handkerchief and explained how they had received his letter, and had then found that the box was missing. She burst into tears again. "All your gold is gone!"

"Not gold, my dear." Jim smiled wryly at her. "A fifty-pound Bank of England note."

The fact that it was not gold which had been lost made Alison feel a little better. She dried her eyes and tried to smile. Then she heard Johnnie's feet on the stairs.

"Allie! Allie!" He burst in the door and stopped dead when he saw Jim.

"What is it, Johnnie?"

"I . . ." Johnnie remained tongue-tied, looking at Jim.

"This is my Uncle, Jim Ashburn, Johnnie, father's friend."

"What's the news?" said Jim.

"Allie. Your Mam's been took by the police!" Alison gasped.

"Took?" said Jim.

"Yes! For stealing a fifty-pound note!"

Alison sat down and began to cry bitterly. Johnnie put his arm round her to try to comfort her, but he was almost in tears himself.

"What's going to happen to Mrs Jessop?" asked Jim, who was pacing up and down the room.

"Well, *boys* is took to the lock-up," said Johnnie. "And I reckon it's the same for old people too."

"Poor Mammy!" said Alison.

"Then tomorrow," continued Johnnie, going pale at the thought, "she'll be took before the magistrates, and the police will say what happened at the pawn shop, and if there's anyone who has a grudge against her, well that's when they'll come forward and speak."

"But nobody has a grudge against Mammy!"

"It's ridiculous," exclaimed Jim.

"Well, if she's cleared, then they'll let her go, but if she isn't, then she'll go to prison."

"But she hasn't done anything!" protested Alison.

"There, there, your Mammy will be all right. Don't you worry. I'll go down to the lock-up and see what I can do." Jim patted Alison's head kindly.

"I'll come too!" Alison jumped to her feet.

"No, no, you wait here. The chances are they won't let me see her tonight, and even if they do, she'll be much happier to know you're safe at home in bed. Take care of her, Johnnie!" And Jim put on his hat and hurried away. Downstairs, Mr Cleaver was lounging by the kitchen door.

"Oh yes, you're the bloke as give my little girl a bit of mutton pie," he said. He tried to smile, but as his teeth were very bad and a lot of them were missing, the effect was not very pleasant.

"Bess? Yes – she was hungry." Jim took a step backwards from the dirty, unkempt man.

"What's this about Mrs Jessop being took for thieving, eh?" asked Mr Cleaver, still smiling.

"There's some mistake." Jim tried to go out, but Mr Cleaver was blocking the doorway.

"You could'a knocked me down with a feather when I 'eard that decent body was took by the police," called Mrs Cleaver across the kitchen.

Mr Cleaver came up close to Jim. "You think she done nothing then?" he whispered.

Jim took another three steps back and said loudly: "Her husband was my greatest friend, and I would trust her in anything."

Mr Cleaver chuckled and winked. "It's easy for a woman to be honest when she's got a husband to look after her."

"What's that you say?" shouted Mrs Cleaver across the kitchen. "Fat lot of looking after *you* do. And who's the honest one round here, I'd like to know?" She could have said a lot more on the subject, but her husband shook his fist at her in a very unpleasant way, and she shrugged her shoulders and took herself off.

"Mrs Jessop," said Jim, keeping his temper with difficulty, "is as honest as they come."

"I'm not saying she isn't," retorted Cleaver. "But she's a widder, and she's desperate hard pinched. And it 'as struck me that she's 'ad something on her mind recently. She's 'ad a real shady look about her . . ."

"I expect she was worrying about her child, and thinking of her husband . . ." Jim sighed, as he remembered his old friend, who now lay under a grassy mound with the sea breezes blowing over him. "Poor Jessop!" he said. "Well, I won't stay here to listen to tales about his widow, so I shall bid you goodnight." He pushed past Cleaver and went out into the courtyard.

Cleaver spat on the floor where Jim had been standing. Then he shambled over to his corner by the fire.

It was very late and very quiet. The children were all asleep, and even the fire was sinking low, with just a few coals glowing red. A hungry-looking mouse ventured out from a hole in the skirting board and foraged for crumbs. The man sat so still and silent that the little creature came right up and scuttled about on the hearthrug.

But Mr Cleaver was not asleep. His mind was working furiously. As the last remnants of the fire died down, he got to his feet and, moving very silently for such a large and ungainly man, tiptoed into the next room. There the youngest children were sleeping, all huddled together on one big mattress. The room was full of the sound of their soft breathing. On a little rickety bed by the wall Bess was tucked up with the baby next to her. Cleaver crept across the room and peered through the open door into his own bedroom. Mrs Cleaver was deeply asleep with her mouth open, sprawled across a large sagging bed. She looked as if nothing could possibly rouse her.

Cleaver went back to Bess and shook her arm. Her eyes opened at once, and she was about to speak. He clapped a hand over her mouth quickly.

"Get up. And don't wake that baby," he whispered, moving his lips, but making hardly any sound at all.

Bess understood him. She slid from under the covers and followed him into the dark kitchen, where the fire was completely out. "I'm cold . . ." she whimpered.

"Shut it," hissed her father fiercely. He gripped her arm tightly. "See this?" He held up a silver coin in front of her face.

"It's a bent sixpence! That means luck!" Bess looked longingly at it. She rarely even saw a whole sixpence, much less had one of her own.

"It's yours if you do what I tells you to . . ." he whispered in her ear, so close that his whiskers scratched her cheek. "First thing. You got to swear you won't peach. Don't tell no one what I'm asking you to do."

"I swear," said Bess, looking at the sixpence.

"You know what a broken bone is?" Cleaver tightened

his grip on her arm so that she winced. "Well, if you peaches on me that's what you'll get." He twisted her arm.

"Ouch! I won't tell!" Bess tried to squirm away from her father.

"Now then," he continued, "if Mrs Jessop gets cleared tomorrow and she comes home, that sailor chappie'll be hanging round trying to find out who's took 'is bleeding tin box, won't 'e? Well, we don't want no strangers hovering round this place do we? So this is what you're going to do. You're going to come along with me tomorrow and tell that story about the box."

"What story?"

"The one what you heard Mrs Jessop tell about it being stole. But you're going to make out that she was real frightened about it. Frightened the sailor chappie would have her put in prison . . ."

Suddenly Bess did not care about the sixpence so much. "She wasn't frightened, Father."

"But you've got to drop the hint, see? You got to make out she was always hiding in corners, and wouldn't look no one in the face." Cleaver slackened his grip and gave his daughter an awkward pat on the head. "You're a smart one Bess. You can do it. Make out you're real sorry for her. But if she goes to prison, you get this . . ." he held up the sixpence again . . . "and if she doesn't go to prison you get *this*." He twisted her arm again and then shoved her back into the bedroom.

Bess crawled back into bed, and lay nursing her sore arm. She could not go back to sleep again. When the light began to show behind the old blanket pinned across the window, she got up, sneaked past her snoring father in the kitchen, and ran upstairs. Johnnie was sleeping outside Alison's door, wrapped in a blanket. Bess stepped over him and went inside.

"Oh . . ." said Alison, opening her eyes and seeing Bess leaning over the bed. "What is it?" Then she remembered. "Oh, my Mammy!"

"Yes," said Bess, looking scornfully at the half-asleep Alison. "Poor sort of watchdog you got! I stepped right over our Johnnie, and he didn't even blink an eyelid."

"What is it, Bess?" Alison rubbed her eyes.

"I was just a-thinking. 'Bout your Mammy. D'you reckon she loves me?"

"Perhaps," said Alison, surprised. Then she added bravely: "She'll be home today."

"She kissed me, didn't she? No one else ever done that before. And she give me that egg and bread." Bess looked round at the little room, at the bright china and the few other treasures from the cottage by the sea. Then she jumped to her feet. She ran to the door, then ran back and gave Alison a quick hug. Then she was gone, and Alison heard Johnnie yell with pain and surprise as his sister kicked him on her way downstairs.

Alison jumped out of bed and searched for her best clothes. Everything was old, and most of her clothes were too small, but they were clean and neatly-mended. She brushed and combed her hair, and called to Johnnie.

"We must go!" she said. "I've got to see Mammy."

Johnnie stumbled in, rubbing his eyes and peered out of the window. "It's hardly light yet. You won't be able to get in. The courts won't be open."

Alison was longing to get away, but she waited and made a cup of tea for Johnnie. She even managed to eat a little of the loaf left over from the night before. Then they set out for the courtroom.

Chapter Six

The court was in a large gloomy building in one of the main streets. There were a lot of people pushing to get inside, and a policeman was standing on guard.

"What's happening?" whispered Alison.

"They're queuing up to go in and watch," said Johnnie. "Some of them 'as relatives being tried, and some of them just wants a bit of fun." Alison shivered. Suddenly a hand plucked Johnnie's coat. He looked round quickly. "Bess! What are you doing here?" But Bess ran away and dodged out of sight round the corner of the building. "Wait here, Alison. I must see what she wants," said Johnnie, and he raced after Bess. "What is it Bess?"

"Shush!" Bess put a finger to her lips and looked round anxiously. "It's Father! He'll be here any minute and he'll be looking for me."

"Why?"

"Because he's dead against Mrs Jessop!" In a breathless whisper Bess told her brother about what had happened in the kitchen the night before. "I ain't a-going to help him," she said, "she was real good to me and I ain't going to put her in prison. I'm going to run away for a bit till Father's cooled down. But if I come back tonight and wait round that corner by the public house, will you come and tell me what happens?"

"Oh Bess, you should never've told a thing like that to Father," whispered Johnnie. "But I'll come. Now get back in the shadows or Father'll see you." He ran back to Alison, who was just about to go in through the big doors, and was looking round anxiously for him.

"Aren't there a lot of people?" she whispered, as they sat down on a hard wooden bench in the court.

Johnnie could see his father sitting in front of them. He

kept twisting his head and looking around with a fierce scowl. Johnnie didn't say anything about what Bess had told him. Instead he tried to distract Alison's attention.

"Look – that gent there is from the pawn shop."

"And I think that lady sitting next to him is the cook from the house where Mammy works. But where's Uncle Jim?" asked Alison.

Johnnie's sharp eyes ranged round the courtroom. "He's just come in. Up there, look."

Mr Cleaver noticed Jim Ashburn too, and muttered something to himself. He stopped looking round for Bess, and sat facing straight ahead with his shoulders hunched.

As the court filled up, the noise of people chattering and arguing and the clatter of their feet on the boards grew deafening. Then there was a loud banging noise and everyone went quiet and stood up. A man in a long black gown came into court from the side, and another man walked behind him.

"That's the magistrate," whispered Johnnie.

Alison was very bewildered and couldn't quite tell what was happening. Then she heard her mother's name called. Mrs Jessop walked in with a policeman beside her and went to stand in a raised wooden box, which Johnnie said was called the dock. Alison waved, but Mrs Jessop did not wave back, she just looked at Alison and gave a little nod to show she had seen. Alison began to feel very nervous. The palms of her hands were damp with sweat and she hoped she was not going to be sick.

Mrs Jessop stood in the dock and answered a lot of questions. Then other people got up and were questioned. Alison heard her name called.

"Go on," hissed Johnnie in her ear. "Go and tell them all what you know!"

"I can't!"

"You must! It looks bad if you don't get up and speak."

Johnnie pushed Alison to her feet, and with trembling legs she made her way to the front of the court. All the people's eyes were fixed on her, and their faces looked like a great swaying sea. Alison swallowed nervously. But the magistrate was a kindly man. He saw that she was frightened and tried to put her at her ease. "Don't worry about anyone else, my dear," he said. "Just try to answer me."

Alison looked up at the magistrate, swallowed again, and answered his questions about who she was and where she lived.

"And you say you saved your pennies to buy a warm petticoat for your mammy?" he asked.

"Yes sir." Alison explained that her mother didn't mind things being old-fashioned so long as they were well-made and warm. A murmur of approval went round the court. People nodded and whispered to each other: "Poor little soul!" One or two smiled at Alison.

Then she sat down again, and Mr Hynes stood up. "I would like to point out, sir," he said, "that this petticoat was in my shop for a number of years, and if a fifty-pound note was concealed in the hem, then in all fairness I would think that the fifty pounds belongs to me."

"Findings keepings!" shouted a loud voice from the back of the court. There was a roar of laughter, and Mr Hynes was promptly ushered out by a policeman. The magistrate banged on his desk, with a little hammer.

Then the cook stepped in to give evidence.

"Mrs Jessop is a fine worker and never gives no trouble. I ain't never missed nothing from the kitchen all the time she was working there," she said.

"I thought she had a nice face," whispered Alison.

The magistrate was banging his little hammer again. "It seems to me," he began, "that no real evidence has been brought against the woman Jessop. All have testified to her good character . . ."

There was a sudden disturbance in the courtroom. "You ain't heard me yet!" shouted Mr Cleaver.

"If you have anything to say, come forward and be sworn."

Alison looked at Johnnie in bewilderment as Mr Cleaver stumbled forward. As he took the oath, Cleaver scowled and kept looking round for Bess. "We are waiting to hear what you have to say," said the magistrate.

"Well," began Mr Cleaver, giving Bess up as a bad job, "my little girl, what should have been here with me now, but ain't, she telled me a very queer thing."

"Come to the point!"

"She heard Mrs Jessop tell *her* little girl – the one as you have just heard – that a sailor bloke 'ad left a tin box full of money to be looked after by the widder . . ."

A great gasp of astonishment went round the court. Alison's name was called again, and she had to go and answer a lot more questions.

"Do you remember what was in that box, Alison Jessop?"

"Uncle Jim's savings."

"Was your mother *afraid* when she knew Ashburn was coming to collect his box?"

"Well, she was upset . . ."

"Upset?"

"For Uncle Jim, who had lost his box . . ."

The magistrate asked: "Was she afraid that Ashburn might suspect her of stealing the box?"

Alison was beginning to get confused, and could not remember very clearly what had happened. "I don't know," she said.

"What was in the box?" the question came again.

"I told you! Uncle Jim's savings! Fifty pounds."

There was a murmur in the courtroom, and people's faces did not look so friendly now. The magistrate frowned and looked through his notes. Jim stood up and made his way forward.

"May I speak?" he said. He took the oath and got up in the witness box. "I only want to say," he began, "that if my mate's widow finds fifty pounds in the hem of a petticoat – well why shouldn't it be there? It may well be the fashion for ladies to keep their money in such places." There was a roar of laughter at this. "And this humbugging story dragged in about my box! I ain't going to bother her about that money and I don't see why anyone else should. She's a sight more honest than anyone else in this court. That's my right hand –" he held it up – "and you may cut it off if you find that the widow Jessop is a thief!"

Johnnie let out a cheer. But the magistrate was still frowning and leafing through his notes. He began to make his final summing up. Alison was feeling much happier now that Jim had spoken up for her mother, but the magistrate's tone was not a happy one.

"The coincidence of a fifty-pound note being lost, and a fifty-pound note being allegedly found by the widow Jessop, would seem to stretch belief too far. Fifty-pound notes do not grow on trees. I have no option but to commit Jessop for trial at the next assizes."

"Not fair!" shouted Jim.

Mrs Jessop was very pale. She was holding tightly on to the side of the dock. "Sir, I am quite innocent, and I am sure that my innocence will be proved eventually. But my little girl, may I have a word with her?"

"Five minutes, Jessop, in the presence of a constable."

Mrs Jessop was lead out of the courtroom by the door at the side. As Alison and Johnnie went out, there was a lot of whispering in the court and people turned round to look at them. In the corridor, another policeman beckoned Alison into a little side room. Her mother was inside.

"Mammy!" Alison hugged her mother tightly. "You

didn't steal it!"

"Oh dearie me!" Mrs Jessop sighed. "Now don't you worry, Allie, I'll be all right. But I don't know what you are going to do, I'm sure. You've no money, you don't know how to earn, how will you live?"

"I'd rather die than be without you!" said Alison.

Just then Jim stepped into the room. "I'll take care of her," he said. "I'm strong, and I'm willing to work. I'll see that your little girl don't starve. She'll be my little girl till you come back." Mrs Jessop began to cry with relief. "This is a disgraceful business," he said, "and I won't leave a stone unturned until we've set you free."

"Bless you Jim!" said Mrs Jessop.

"And I'll get her dinner!" It was Johnnie, peering round the door.

"Thank you Johnnie," said Mrs Jessop. She tried to loosen Alison's hold on her.

"I won't leave you! I'll stay with you! Let me stay!" cried Alison, clinging even tighter.

"No, Allie. You must be brave. Show you are a sailor's daughter."

"That's right," said Jim. "A sailor's daughter, and a sailor to watch out for you." He took Alison's hand. "You and me has got our work cut out now to find the thief who took my box."

"And me!" said Johnnie. "I'll 'elp yer!"

Very reluctantly Alison let Jim lead her away. She did not want the policeman who was standing in the room to see her cry. But as Mrs Jessop blew her a kiss, and the policeman went to shut the door to separate them, she burst into tears.

"Now then!" said Jim, getting out his big red handkerchief and mopping her eyes. "You've got a plucky mammy, and you must be the same. Come home now, and dry your eyes."

Chapter Seven

Mr Cleaver arrived home that evening in a black temper. He was angry and tired and very much in need of a drink.

"Well some folks can sing!" he shouted at his wife, who was humming to herself as she ironed the clean washing.

"The bad penny's turned up again I see," she remarked, thumping the iron down on the smooth linen.

"I wish I had a penny," muttered Cleaver. Johnnie's little brother Jos who was rocking the baby's cradle moved back out of his father's way.

"Drink, drink, drink. You'll drink yourself into the grave. And a nice relief that'll be for us all."

"I don't want no lecture," snapped Cleaver, and slouched to his chair. His wife went on working. When the iron she was using began to get cool, she changed it for one of the others which were heating by the fire, and the rhythmic thump and swish continued. She had been thinking about Mrs Jessop all day, and after a pause she asked her husband what had happened. He told her.

"What!" she exclaimed, letting the iron rest still for a moment. "You could have spoken up for her! If I hadn't been stuck here with all these kids and piles of washing to do, I'd have gone and said a good word."

Cleaver grunted. "Where's Bess?" he asked.

Mrs Cleaver ignored him. She snatched up the iron – which was just about to burn a hole – and went on with her work. "Poor decent soul," she said. "She's no more stole than I have! You've no ounce of heart left in that great dirty body of yours."

"Don't you let your words out on me!" Cleaver threatened his wife with his large fist. "Where's our Bess? She's angered me proper. I want her."

"Oh, leave her alone!"

"I'll break every bone in 'er body when I catches her!"

"Ain't you ashamed to call yourself a father?" With the heavy iron in her hand and the ironing table between them, Mrs Cleaver was not worried by her husband's threats.

"I want that girl! Where've you hid her?"

"I don't know nothing about her, and I haven't seen her for hours. She's a lazy piece. That baby's been screaming its head off half the time."

"Hey!" Mr Cleaver got to his feet as Johnnie and Alison came in. "Where's our Bess?" Johnnie stood for a moment with his hands in his pockets.

"Er – ain't she here?"

"No, she ain't." Mr Cleaver approached menacingly. He stopped dead when he saw Jim standing in the doorway.

"Good day," said Jim quietly.

"Is that Alison?" called Mrs Cleaver. She left the ironing and welcomed Alison with a damp hug. "There, there, my pet. God's watching over your mammy, you take it from me, he's watching over her." Alison emerged limply from the hug. She was feeling very miserable indeed. Jim spoke quietly to Mrs Cleaver.

"I've promised Mrs Jessop to keep any eye on Alison. But I'll be getting some work, and I'll be glad if you'd see that she's all right when I'm away."

"Oh *yes!* She's more than welcome to come down here any time of day or night," said Mrs Cleaver, preparing to give Alison another hug. "You can rock the baby's cradle for me can't you?" Alison thanked her and backed away.

"And I'll get your dinner, don't forget!" said Johnnie, and would have followed them upstairs but his mother called him back to deliver some washing.

Later on that evening after Jim had gone, Alison sat on her

little stool, staring into the red heart of the fire. Everything was very quiet and still, and it was now getting dark. Then there was a heavy step on the stair and a loud knock at the door. Before she could move, the door opened and Cleaver's head came round it. He smiled at her, which made him look even more frightening than usual. "You got Bess in here?" he asked. Alison shook her head.

"She's a-hiding somewhere," he said, and Alison was terrified that he was going to come in and search under the bed and in the cupboards. She sat still and said nothing, and after a moment he went away. He banged the door behind him, and the stairs creaked under his weight as he went down.

It was silent again, except for the baby's cry which could be heard faintly. At last Alison heard the sound she had been longing to hear; Johnnie's whistle as he leaped up the stairs two at a time.

"All ship-shape, Matie?" he said, as he came in, trying to do a sailor's salute.

"All ship-shape, Captain," she replied.

"Did Father frighten you?"

"A bit," Alison shivered.

"He wants a drink," said Johnnie, sitting on a little stool by the fire, "and he can't get the money for one."

"He should work!" said Alison.

"But if he works," said Johnnie, "then he spends the money getting drunk! I don't know what's worse, him with money getting drunk, or him without money giving us gyp." He reached up for the big shell on the mantelshelf and listened to it. "Still there, that old sea. How d'you reckon it gets into the shell, Allie?"

"It creeps in when the shell is floating in the sea." Alison watched him holding the shell to his ear in the flickering firelight. "Where is Bess?" she asked.

"I can't tell you, Allie. But I'm going to see her now,

she's all right."

"Can I come too?"

"No, it's not safe."

"But I don't like sitting here on my own thinking about you."

"All right then. But you musn't tell no one you've seen her. Father's mad to get his hands on her. He wanted Bess to go to court and say that your mother was a thief. But she wouldn't go."

Alison got her coat and hat. "But why does he want Mammy in prison?" she asked. "How has she harmed him?"

"I dunno," Johnnie shrugged. "I reckon he hates her 'cos she's good."

The alley by the courtroom was now very dark, although the gas lamp on the corner made a little pool of yellowish light in the gloom.

"Bess?" whispered Johnnie.

"I thought you was never coming!" A white face appeared from the shadows. "What d'you bring her for?" she demanded as she saw Alison.

"I was lonely, Bess." said Alison. Her teeth were chattering in the cold night air.

"Lonely?" Bess peered at her.

"My Mammy . . . "

"Ain't she home then?"

"Father spoke bad on her, Bess," whispered Johnnie.

Bess was tired and cold and cross. "I might just as well have gone there and spoke up like Father wanted! I could have had that sixpence and not been starved and cold out here." Johnnie pushed a piece of bread into her hand.

"Careful!" he said. "Mind your teeth. There's a penny in the middle to buy you some coffee."

"Thank you for not telling those lies about my

Mammy," said Alison.

"I couldn't hurt her, could I? Not after she give me all them things." Bess munched her bread. "I didn't do no good, though, did I? Father managed it on his own."

"You'd better not come back to the house for a while, Bess. He's still angry," said Johnnie. "You can sleep in one of the cellars. We'll get some straw for you to lie on."

They made their way slowly back to Adler's Court, going a long way round to avoid the public house. Bess was chilled to the bone from being outside all evening, and kept complaining about the cold. They stopped at a little stall to buy her some hot coffee, and Alison took off her woollen shawl and put it round Bess's shoulders. "I won't forget your goodness, and I'll tell Mammy. You shall have my shawl to keep you warm in the cellar."

They tiptoed back into the dark courtyard, keeping well clear of the Cleavers' kitchen door. Johnnie led them over to an opening which led down to the cellars and under the houses. It was covered over with half-rotten boards. When he tried to push them aside, they creaked loudly, and the three children froze for a long time. No one seemed to have heard, and there was no sound of approaching foot-steps.

"Somebody's tried to block up the entrance," whispered Johnnie. "All the better for us!" He managed to shift a plank and make a little gap, and they crept inside. They felt their way down the rough stone steps in the dark, clinging to the wall as they went. The stones were damp and icy to the touch, and Alison shivered with cold and fear. When they reached the bottom they were in complete darkness.

"Careful!" exclaimed Johnnie, as Alison bumped into him. He fumbled in his pocket and got out a bit of tallow candle which he lit.

"Everything to hand, as the legless wonder said," he

joked. Bess began to giggle. He quietened her and held up the little flame as he walked around the cellar, lighting up a broken bedstead, some chair legs, lots of bottles and boxes and a heap of old straw.

"You'll be quite comfy here Bess." Johnnie stuck the candle on top of an old box and began to spread out the straw. "This isn't a bit damp. Must have been brought down not so long ago."

There was a creak and a scuffle at the top of the stairs. Alison jumped. Johnnie dived at the candle and clapped his hand over the flame. His fingers hurt for a moment, but the light was extinguished at once. There was more scuffling from the top of the stairs, and a muffled exclamation.

"Steady now . . ." they heard. It was Cleaver's voice, and he was trying to make his way down. Quickly, in the dark, Johnnie pushed the two girls across the cellar to a little door.

"You can get through into the next cellar," he whispered. He was about to follow them when he heard a match being struck. As the flickering light shone on the walls he dropped down flat and crouched behind the broken bedstead.

"Blessed rats . . ." muttered Cleaver to himself. He lit a small candle, and set it on the ground. His eyes were not yet used to the dark, and he did not see Johnnie. He went across to the pile of straw, kicked it aside, and scraped at the black earth underneath with his foot. Then he got out his large clasp knife and dug out large lumps of soil with it. Johnnie peered round the end of the bedstead to try to discover what he was doing. He saw his father lift out a small box from the hole he had dug.

As his father held it up in the candle-light, Johnnie saw a painted picture on top of the box, and a padlock. His father didn't touch the padlock, but opened the box from the back, and Johnnie saw that the hinges had been smashed. He took out an envelope, opened it, and pored greedily over the contents. Johnnie craned his neck to see. His father was holding a fifty-pound note in his hand.

Cleaver sat back on his haunches after a while and grumbled to himself: "What the hell use is it to me? I try to change it and where am I? In the clink with Mrs Jessop! Not blooming likely!" He folded up the note and stuffed it back in the box. "Wish it had 'a' bin gold. I could've changed it bit by bit." He was just putting the box back in the earth when Johnnie stepped forward and touched him on the shoulder.

Cleaver was on his feet with his knife in his hand in a split second. "You little spy!" Johnnie did not move. "Don't look at me that way," said Cleaver, lowering the knife and wiping his forehead. "You nearly killed me with the fright!"

"Come away, Father," said Johnnie. "Come out of this before folks find you." Mr Cleaver thought that an excellent idea. He picked up the candle and followed Johnnie up into the courtyard. Alison, trembling with fear, flitted after them and flattened herself against the wall nearby.

"You seen what I done!" hissed Cleaver to his son. "Don't you think you're very mean, spying on your father like that?"

"I don't know what I thinks," replied Johnnie miserably.

"Well, what's done is done, and can't be helped, can it?" Cleaver said. Johnnie moved away and did not reply. "You just got to keep a quiet tongue in your head, and no harm will come to nobody." Johnnie still did not answer. Cleaver began to relax. "Has you tuppence or threepence about you?" he asked. "I'm desperate for two penn'orth of gin."

"I hasn't any money."

"Ah well . . ." Cleaver shrugged and made as if to go.

"Father, I can't keep quiet!" Johnnie spoke up quickly. His father turned back and grabbed him by the coat sleeve.

"Ain't I your father what has to be obeyed?" he said, glaring into Johnnie's face.

"I can't let Mrs Jessop lie in prison for what you done! And I can't let that sailor man go without his money. It ain't right."

Mr Cleaver was red with rage. "You'll tell on your own father?" he shouted. "You're unnatural! You deserves to be thrashed to an inch of your life!" He shook Johnnie viciously.

"I didn't say I'd . . . tell on you. . . . Father," gasped Johnnie breathlessly. "But I must take the box back to . . . Mr Ashburn. No one need know it was . . . you . . . took it!"

"They'd be certain positive to guess." Cleaver twisted Johnnie's arm. "They'll take me up and put me in prison." He slackened his hold and began to plead with Johnnie. "I can't lie in prison! I can't! Think what it'd do to me. Never a drop of drink in all the time I'm there." Johnnie stared at him. "I was always fond of you Johnnie. More than the others. You was my firstborn! You wouldn't want me in prison a-dying for the want of a drink, would you?"

Johnnie didn't know what to think. He couldn't help feeling a bit sorry for his father, who was obviously terrified, but he couldn't forget that Mrs Jessop was in prison.

"Why don't you run off if you're frightened of being taken?" he said.

"Where would I go? How would I live? I ain't got no money."

"You could work . . ."

"I can't get work, can I? You're very unfeeling, Johnnie." Cleaver paused for a moment, eyeing his son's face. "Look, let it lie over for a week, eh? Promise me you won't tell no one what you seen in the cellar, just for a week."

"And at the end of a week?"

"Well then – you may do as you please. D'you hear me?"

"Yes father. I promise to do nothing for a week."

"There's my good lad. A week won't make much difference to no one." Cleaver put his arm round his son's shoulders and they went into the house together.

Chapter Eight

"Johnnie!" whispered Alison from the darkness at the foot of the stairs.

"Allie!" Johnnie went to her quickly. "Are you all right? Did you get out through the other cellar?"

"Bess did. I waited for you."

"I said for you to go!"

"I was afraid. I thought you might be hurt."

Johnnie bit his lip. "Did you see. . . ?"

"I saw your father dig up a box. It was Uncle Jim's box, wasn't it?" Johnnie nodded.

"What are we going to do?" asked Alison.

"You're not going to do anything. It's up to me."

"But what about Mammy? In prison."

"Well, I can't just let my Father go to prison, can I?"

"No, I suppose not," said Alison.

"Just give me a bit of time to think what's best to do," said Johnnie.

"I'll try to think of something too," said Alison. "He won't hurt you will he?"

"No, he won't hurt me. Go up to bed now. It's very late. I'll look after everything, don't worry."

Alison tiptoed up to her room, feeling her way along the wall in the dark.

Next morning when Alison opened the door Johnnie fell into the room at her feet. He had spent the night asleep on the landing, leaning back on the door. He blinked at her, then grinned and sat up. His grin faded when he saw Bess sitting up in the little bed.

"Bess, what are you doing up here?"

"Shush!" whispered Alison. "I said she could stay."

"But Father . . . "

"I can hide in the cupboard if he comes up. I couldn't stay in them cellars! They're scary, and perishing cold."

"She's company for me, Johnnie," said Alison.

"Well, it won't be for long," said Johnnie. "Then you can walk in on Ma as bold as brass."

Bess looked worried. "Won't father wallop me? I ain't a-feared of most things, but I couldn't bear to hear my bones cracking."

"There'll be nothing to fear, Bess, you'll see." Johnnie picked up the heavy iron kettle. "I'll go down and get the water, Allie. It's too heavy for you when it's full." He went down to the courtyard, filled the kettle at the pump, and carried it back up the stairs.

"Don't you let that slop all over the place," shouted his mother after him. "And come back down 'ere when you've done. I've got things to say to you."

When Johnnie got back to the kitchen his mother started right away. "All these carryings-on!" she said. "If you turn against your duties, you'll never prosper, Johnnie. Mark my words, you'll get like your father, drinking all day."

"I ain't turning against my duties," said Johnnie miserably. "It's just . . ." He couldn't explain about finding the box or about his promise to his father, so he went to do some mangling, turning the stiff handle so fast that it creaked and groaned.

"I don't know! Gadding about all hours of the night! What are you up to, that's what I'd like to know. . . ." muttered Mrs Cleaver.

Little Jos came to help him, and did his best to fold up the clothes when they had been wrung out. He had a lot of trouble as his arms were much too short. Johnnie laughed at him. "See, Jos – first you fold it longways, then you fold it sideways, then you get it by the short hairs . . ." Jos roared with laughter as Johnnie showed him how to fold up a big sheet.

"Johnnie!" shouted Mrs Cleaver. "Stop that! Putting your work on to Jos! He can't be expected to do it. Go and play, Jos." Jos began to cry, and went out into the courtyard, dragging his feet. Then the baby began to wail.

"Oh lord!" sighed Mrs Cleaver, pushing the cradle with her foot. "I got too much to do. Your father's getting more unnatural every day. I thought drink broke a man's health – but his appetite! He eats like a horse."

"If you hadn't got him to support," said Johnnie slowly, "lounging around all day and eating his head off, I suppose you'd have an easier time of it."

"Johnnie!" exclaimed Mrs Cleaver. "Your father's a worry, but I shouldn't want to see him dead. If that's your hard-hearted thought then I'm ashamed of you!"

"He ain't a-going to die, Mother," said Johnnie, turning the handle of the mangle faster than ever. The baby roared an accompaniment to the noise of the mangle.

"And where's our Bess?" said Mrs Cleaver, giving the cradle a shove. "The way he rates at her I don't know what she's done to him. But I wish she'd come back and see to this baby."

"She'll be back soon."

"I hope she hasn't took to thieving. She were always a pert one. I can't a-bear that my children should take to bad ways. It's desperate hard for poor folks to see a way ahead." She went on with her washing, pounding and kneading the clothes in the tub.

She need not have worried, for Bess was safe upstairs with Alison. The time passed very slowly in the little room. Johnnie was kept busy helping his mother downstairs, and could only pop up occasionally with a plate of pudding or a pie for their dinner. Jim was busy too. He had got himself a labouring job at the docks, and most days he was too tired to stay for more than a few minutes when he called round in the evenings to make sure Alison was all right.

Alison got her work basket out one morning and tried to teach Bess how to mend her clothes. Bess had never held a needle in her life, but she was determined to succeed, and at the end of a week she was good enough to be able to darn a huge hole in one of her stockings. Alison inspected it with a critical eye.

"That's quite good, Bess. It's a bit knobbly, but you are getting better." Johnnie's whistle sounded outside, and Alison jumped up to let him in.

"You ain't half soft you two," said Bess scornfully. But when Johnnie came in he was looking pale and serious, and not like his usual self at all.

"You look like you lost a tanner and found a ha'penny," said his sister rudely.

"I thought you had given us up, Johnnie. Where've you been?" said Alison.

"I been busy."

"You know Mammy's trial comes up in a fortnight?" Alison gave him a meaningful look.

"I'm sure she'll be set free," said Johnnie. But he did not sound very happy. He picked up the shell and listened to it for a moment.

"Aren't you well, Johnnie?" asked Alison. "You look so pale."

"I'm just miserable, Allie."

"Ain't we all," chipped in Bess.

"But I'm happy too." Johnnie made a brave attempt to cheer himself up. He put the shell back and touched the silver trumpet for luck. "Look out for Bess, won't you Allie?"

"What's the matter Johnnie? Where are you going?"

"I can look after myself thank you very much," said Bess crossly, concentrating on a large hole in her stocking.

Johnnie signalled Alison to keep quiet. "Tell your mother to say a good word to her," he continued.

"You sound like you was off to Africa tomorrow," said Bess, looking up for a moment.

"Hello there, anyone home?" Jim's step was heard on the landing.

"Mutton pies!" said Bess, sniffing rapturously.

"How many of us are there?" asked Jim, coming in and setting the pies on the table. "Four?"

"I don't fancy no pies," said Johnnie.

"Don't you feel well?"

"I'm all right," said Johnnie. He slipped out and ran downstairs before there were any more questions.

Much later that night Johnnie took a candle and went down into the cellars again. He crouched in the corner by the pile of straw and scrabbled at the earth until he could pull out the tin box. He hurried up from the cellar with the box clasped to his chest.

In the little room at the top of the stairs, Bess and Alison were fast asleep. They did not stir when Johnnie put the box on the table beside the bed. On his way down again he passed through the kitchen and went into his mother's room. She lay asleep, snoring gently with the baby in the crook of her arm. Johnnie had a knotted handkerchief in his pocket with some of the small change he had earned on the street corner by the pawn shop. He laid it on her pillow, and tiptoed out before she woke.

He made his way to the public house by the courtroom. Although it was very late, the shouting and singing of the people inside could be heard a long way off. Light spilled from its windows over the pavements, and every now and then a drunken man staggered out and wove his way along the pavement. Johnnie found himself a dark corner and waited patiently until Mr Cleaver emerged, singing hoarsely to himself. He stumbled about and leaned against a lamp-post as a couple walked past him arm in arm. Johnnie stepped out of the shadows and plucked at his coat sleeve.

"What's that?" grunted Cleaver.

"It's me, Father!"

"Can't talk to you t'night." Cleaver belched. "I'm dead tired."

"Father, you promised!" Cleaver tried to throw off Johnnie's hold on his arm, and staggered clumsily across the pavement. "I'll talk to you tomorrow," he said.

"No, no," said Johnnie. "You don't understand. I dug up the box and I've given it to Alison."

"You done that? I'd like to kill you!" Cleaver gave Johnnie a shake, then staggered unsteadily. Johnnie had to hold him up or he would have fallen.

"I've got an idea. We can go somewhere a long way off where no one could find you."

"We?"

"I'll stand by you Father. I'll get you food and lodging and a drop to drink."

Cleaver laughed. "You?" he said.

"I've got a shilling in my pocket as I earned, and I can earn more like that."

Cleaver was still scornful. "Let's see the colour of your money then," he said. "Show us the bob you earned so honest."

Johnnie clutched the shilling which was deep in his pocket. "No. Come on Father, let's get away now."

Cleaver hesitated for a moment. Then a little smile dawned on his face. "All right. But I chooses the lodging. I know a nice safe place. Safe from nosey parkering police and such. I've been thinking of moving on, but didn't fancy it on me own like." He took Johnnie's arm. "You come with me and I'll see that you're all right." He led

Johnnie off into the darkness.

They walked very slowly, partly because Mr Cleaver could not keep to a straight course and kept wavering about all over the pavement. It seemed an awfully long way to Johnnie. He noticed that the houses they went past were getting more and more dilapidated. Many of them had boarded-up windows, and there was a lot of rubbish and filth underfoot in the streets. Even Johnnie wrinkled up his nose in disgust at some of the smells that wafted up.

Cleaver was muttering to himself all the way. Suddenly he came to an abrupt halt. He looked up at a street sign in the dull gaslight.

"Queen Street," he said. "Here we are."

"It's a terrible place!" said Johnnie, looking at the mean houses, the dirty street, and breathing in the foul air.

"It's safe," said his father.

"I don't think I can bear it."

"Didn't I tell you it's safe?" hissed Cleaver. "It's that what counts now you've given the game away. Anyway, we're too late to go back now."

Two men lounging against a wall nearby had seen them. One was tall and powerfully built, with a shiny bald head and a flower in his buttonhole. His companion was small and wiry, with slicked-down hair and a scarred face.

"Cleaver, ain't it?" said the larger man.

"There now!" Cleaver peered at him through the gloom. "If it ain't my old friend Mallinger!"

"Was we friends?" The man with the buttonhole looked doubtful. "I suppose in a manner of speaking we was. You moving in?"

"That's what I thought. The bobbies have got it in for me now."

"You always was a fool, Cleaver." The little man spat disdainfully on the ground.

"Shut it Ned. We got a nice apartment all ready for you Cleaver. Just down here." Mallinger indicated a cellar door and kicked it open.

"That'd suit me very well," said Cleaver. They both laughed unpleasantly, but Mallinger was watching Johnnie with interest.

"That your boy? You bringing him to join us?" he asked.

"I can't let him roam on his own, can I?"

"You know that no one comes to Queen Street without paying the piper?" Mallinger dropped his voice and his tone was very serious.

"Oh yes. I know that Mall. Don't you worry. He's a bright, sharp lad, and he'll do his best, won't you?"

"I hope so Father." Johnnie shivered, looking down into the dark cellar.

"We'll see. Show them the apartment, Ned."

Little Ned gave a mocking bow and held the cellar door open for Johnnie and his father. "Mind you don't spoil the furniture!" he shouted after them.

At first Johnnie could see nothing, but when his father lit a candle he gasped in surprise. "There isn't any furniture!"

"Ned's little joke. Look, we got plenty of straw."

"But it's all wet," said Johnnie, looking at the water trickling down the walls.

"Beggars can't be choosers," said his father, and then slumped down on a pile of straw. A moment later he was snoring loudly.

The flickering candle-light made weird shadows on the uneven walls. Then the candle spluttered and died, and the darkness closed in on Johnnie. There were strange scufflings in the straw and he hoped the mice would leave him alone. He had never felt quite so miserable in his whole life.

Chapter Nine

To the inhabitants of Adler's Court, Mr Cleaver and Johnnie seemed to have vanished into thin air. One person who was really pleased by their disappearance was Bess. As soon as she was sure that her father was gone, she left Alison and went back downstairs to her mother.

But her pleasure was short-lived, because as soon as she appeared she was presented with the baby to look after. He seemed to be larger and heavier and noisier than ever. To keep him quiet she carried him to the doorstep and sat with him on her knee.

"Home again?" said Jim, arriving at the kitchen door. He patted her on the head as he squeezed past her.

"Ain't I just," she sighed. "Next time I'm born I'll be a boy. They don't have no truck with babies!"

"Uncle Jim!" Alison could not wait for him to climb the stairs but came racing down to meet him. "Have you heard?"

"What's all the excitement?" he asked.

She held up the tin box.

"Johnnie found it," she said proudly.

"Wait a minute. Johnnie *found* it?" Jim looked suspicious. "How did he find it?"

"Johnnie is as honest as Mammy," said Alison quickly. "He wouldn't steal anything."

Jim had picked up the box and was looking at it closely. He opened the broken hinges, and saw that the fifty-pound note was still inside. "Why take the box and not use the money? Unless – unless they were afraid of being caught." He felt as though he could hardly believe his own eyes.

"Fifty-pound notes don't grow on trees," said Alison, mimicking the magistrate.

Jim laughed. "But where did Johnnie find it?" he asked. "It all seems very odd to me."

"I can't tell you that," replied Alison, and she looked so worried that Jim asked no more questions.

"It looks as though we shall have your Mammy home in no time!" he said, to cheer her up.

"Oh Uncle Jim!" cried Alison, giving him a hug. But she could not help wishing that Johnnie could be there too.

The first day in Queen Street Johnnie got up early and went out. He found a likely-looking street corner and stood there to whistle to the passers-by. But this was a poor area, a long way from the more prosperous parts of town, and the few people who walked past him had no pennies to spare. He walked on to a busier place, but he didn't have much luck. Most of the people looked at him very suspiciously, but one or two were cheered by his tuneful whistling and gave him a smile. All day he went on trying, but at the end he had only six pennies to show for all his efforts.

Meanwhile, Mr Cleaver had been out on a different sort of business. He came back with a loaf and some cheese. He set up an old tea chest as a table and put some boxes to sit on. Then he went out again for a can of hot coffee, so that when Johnnie arrived back cold and tired he was met by the fragrant smell.

"Did you get some work then?" he asked his father.

"Very good work by the looks of it." Cleaver waved the large hunk of bread he was eating. "See this? It's good food this. And we'll soon be out of here. Who knows, we might even be rich!"

"Oh," said Johnnie.

"Draw up a chair," invited Cleaver, shoving one of the boxes towards Johnnie and offering him some cheese on the point of his knife. "You look like you ain't eaten nothing all day."

"I ain't Father," said Johnnie, sitting on the box and eating hungrily.

"Didn't you make no money then?"

"Only this," he said, and laid the six pennies on the table.

"All that whistling for a measly tanner! 'Tain't right. You needs a proper job like me." Cleaver pocketed the six pence.

"What d'you do?"

"Bit here, bit there. You come out with me and I'll learn yer."

There was a clatter of feet on the cellar stairs and the two men who had met them the night before came in, followed by a girl in a tattered dress. Mallinger looked as dapper as ever with a fresh flower in his buttonhole.

"Whose birthday is it?" said the girl, eyeing the food on the table.

"Shut it Poll," Mallinger scowled at her.

"Johnnie, would you mind leaving us for a moment?" said Cleaver, wiping his mouth and staggering to his feet. "There's some things as we have to talk about, so just take your food and clear out." He pushed him up the stairs, but Johnnie stayed just outside the door, eating his bread and cheese.

"What's this?" said Mallinger, helping himself to a piece of cheese. "Still hanging the latch are you? Haven't you spoken to your boy yet? Dear me! We'll have to start charging for the furniture next, won't we?" Ned croaked a little mirthless laugh and Cleaver tried to laugh too, but without much success.

"I done well today Mall," he said eagerly. "I got a wallet and a silver watch." He produced a fistful of money.

"Oooh! Getting his hand in nicely, ain't he!" said the girl with a snigger.

"Shut it, will you Poll." Mallinger took the money. "And what's your lad done? Where's his contribution?"

"I'm a-moving slowly with him," said Cleaver.

"Well that ain't good enough," said Mallinger bluntly. "You've made us promises about that lad."

Johnnie craned his neck and strained his ears to catch what was being said down below him in the cellar. He moved closer to the cellar door and heard his father say: "Don't you worry. I'll have him cracking in no time. I'll make him the best little thief you ever had."

"That's good," said Mallinger. "That's very good indeed. Because if he don't toe the line, then it's all up with you Cleaver. I'll have you cleavered from head to toe!"

Ned chuckled. "Bit messy, Mall."

"He's a likely lad," continued Mallinger, "and if you can't teach him our ways, I'll take him on myself."

Johnnie was creeping further and further forward. Suddenly Poll, who was standing at the foot of the steps, looked up and saw him. Johnnie held his breath, certain that she was going to give him away. But she frowned at him, and signalled him to go away with a jerk of her head.

"What you up to, Poll?" snapped Ned.

"Nothing."

"Then stop it."

"You know the rules here," Mallinger was saying, "we won't touch him, but if he don't show willing within the week, well – we got cellars down here no one knows about save us. And once we put a man in there he never comes out. We could easily put you down there, Cleaver. Remember that."

A few days later Bess staggered into Adler's Court bent almost double under the weight of a huge bag of dirty washing. After a few steps across the courtyard, her legs gave way, and she dropped the bag on the floor.

"Oh – where's that blooming Johnnie!" she muttered to herself. A group of little girls who were playing hopscotch in the courtyard laughed at her. She stuck her tongue out and started dragging the bag towards the kitchen.

"Pick up them clothes, gal!" shouted Mrs Cleaver, coming to the door with the baby on her arm. "You'll have them full of holes! I'll skin that Johnnie when he comes home."

"If he comes home," said Bess, wrestling with the bundle, and trying to arrange it on her back so that none of the clothes were trailing on the ground.

"He'd better." Mrs Cleaver looked hard at Bess. "D'you know where he is?"

"Maybe he's gone with Father." Bess stumbled across the doorstep into the kitchen.

"Well, that's a lot of help seeing as we don't know where he is either!"

"Do you think he *has* gone with Mr Cleaver?" asked Alison who was sitting in the kitchen.

"Learning his drinking ways I reckon," said Bess, and dodged a hefty slap which Mrs Cleaver aimed in her direction.

Alison sighed. She had been waiting all morning to hear from Uncle Jim, who had gone to see Mrs Jessop. It was too lonely to sit in the room upstairs, she did not feel like playing with the other girls outside, and she was far too excited to be of any proper help to Mrs Cleaver. She kept dropping things and forgetting what she had been told just a moment before. So she had been trying to sit still, all the time getting more and more on edge.

Suddenly the girls' voices in the courtyard went quiet. Jim came into the kitchen, blocking out the light from the doorway for a moment. Mrs Jessop was behind him.

"Mammy!" cried Alison. She ran to her and they hugged each other tightly. Mrs Jessop's eyes were shining, and her cheeks were pink.

"Oh it's good to be home!" she said. "How ever did you get on without me, Allie?"

"Well – I suppose I got used to it . . . but it wasn't very nice. Come on up, Mammy, I'll make some tea. I make good tea now."

"You seem quite grown-up!" said Mrs Jessop, as they went upstairs. She hung her hat up on the back of the door and looked around the little room with pleasure.

"I do feel a lot older," said Alison seriously.

"I mustn't go away again, or you'll be an old lady when I come back!" They all laughed. Alison poured some hot water into the teapot.

"Uncle Jim tells me Johnnie's gone away. Is there any news of him?" asked Mrs Jessop.

"No. I've been looking for him," said Alison sadly.

"All on your own?" said Mrs Jessop, looking worried.

"I didn't know about this, Allie!" said Jim.

"I had to look. I looked every day. I kept thinking I'd heard his whistle. Then I'd look and there'd be no one there. He will come back won't he?"

Mrs Jessop shrugged her shoulders. From what Jim had told her she was inclined to be rather suspicious of Johnnie. If it was he who brought the box back, then it was quite likely to be he who had stolen it, and his disappearance seemed to point to the same thing.

"Oh, Mammy!" cried Alison, seeing her mother's face. "He didn't take the box! I promise you he didn't take it! He's not a thief!"

Mrs Jessop changed the subject hastily. "You have been busy," she said, looking round the room. "I can't see a speck of dust anywhere. And this is a lovely cup of tea!"

Alison was very glad indeed to have her mother home again, but as the days passed she found she was missing Johnnie more and more. It was hard not to be able to talk to her mother about him, and she found herself spending more and more time in the busy kitchen downstairs talking to Mrs Cleaver.

Mrs Cleaver was certainly always glad to see her.

"What I needs," she said turning the handle of the mangle until she was red in the face, "is a strong arm to turn this mangle for me while I gets on with me washing."

Alison was not strong enough to turn the handle, but she did her best to help by catching the clean clothes as they fell out of the mangle. Jos had been at it before her, and he had managed to drop far more than he had caught.

"I miss our Johnnie," sighed Mrs Cleaver.

"Yes. He's got a strong arm," said Alison.

"It's not just that. I miss him round the place. I get Bess back, and 'afore I turn round Johnnie's gone!" Seeing Alison's downcast face she added: "There's no need for you to look so sad. You got your Mammy back now."

"Yes," said Alison. "Do you think Johnnie has gone with Mr Cleaver?"

Mrs Cleaver sighed again and looked very worried. "I can guess what's happened," she said. "Cleaver took that box of money, and Johnnie found out. I can guess the whole story." She sniffed and had to stop mangling to wipe her eyes. "Oh my poor Johnnie! I don't think I'll ever see my boy again!" The tears began to run down her cheeks. "He'll starve with that Cleaver! Starve, or something worse."

Alison was horrified to see Mrs Cleaver cry. She forgot that she was holding a clean muslin blouse and crushed it as she clasped her hands together. "We'll find him. We must find him!"

Chapter Ten

Mallinger's words had made a deep impression on Cleaver. He knew he had to press on with Johnnie's "education", as Mallinger called it, but he could not bring himself to tell his son what he was doing. He did not know what Johnnie's reaction would be, but he felt he would not be pleased. So he kept putting it off and putting it off, until one morning he realised it could wait no longer.

"Johnnie! You're coming on out with me this morning," he said.

Johnnie had been expecting this for a long time. He said nothing, and followed his father quietly. Cleaver led him to a crowded place near to the docks. There were many warehouses, with all manner of working men and business men hurrying in and out. Carts were thronging the narrow streets, delivering and collecting bales of goods. Above them cranes and pulleys winched loads up to the top floors of the warehouses and let them down on to waiting carts. Cries of "Look out there," and "Mind yer 'eads!" were heard all the time.

"Keep close by me, and keep yer eyes open," hissed Cleaver to Johnnie, as they dodged round a huge bale of raw cotton being carried by two men.

"Where's the station?" A large fat man in a shiny top hat was looking around in a bewildered way. "Excuse me!" he said, as someone pushing past knocked him against Cleaver. "I'm looking for the railway station. Can you direct me, my man?" Cleaver looked blankly at him.

"Mind yer toes there, gentlemen!" a burly carter was trying to lead his sweating horse along the pavement. The reins were looped up over its back, and its eyes rolled nervously as the crowds pushed round it.

Johnnie moved out of the way of the huge feet and

followed his father who was disappearing rapidly into the crowd.

"Come on matie! Ain't got all bloomin' day!" shouted the carter.

"My watch! Fetch the police! My gold watch has gone!" shouted the fat man.

"Well, don't look at me," the carter was saying rudely, "I've got me work to get to . . ." The great horse squealed and tossed its head and the argument was lost to view as more people crowded round to see what was going on.

"Get a move on," hissed Cleaver. "What you hanging around for? That horse came by in the nick of time. It's our lucky day today!"

Johnnie still said nothing. But he was pretty sure he had seen his father's hand slip into the fat gentleman's pocket. Cleaver was in very good spirits. Johnnie was behaving very well, keeping quiet and watching everything with close attention.

Late that evening he took Johnnie to a second-hand clothes shop near the docks. It was even darker and more dismal than Mr Hynes' shop where Alison had bought the petticoat. There were no clothes here which looked as if they might have belonged to a decent body once. Most of the garments were little better than rags.

A dirty old woman came out to serve them. Without a word she held out her hand. Mr Cleaver held out a beautiful gold watch and a gold propelling pencil. The old woman closed her dirty claw-like hand around them and scrutinised them closely. She hid them under her ragged shawl and counted out twenty shillings on the counter. All this time no word was spoken. Cleaver scooped up the money and hurried out of the shop. "What d'you think of that then?" asked Cleaver proudly as they walked along. He jingled the coins in his pocket. "Let's go and get ourselves a bite of supper."

"I ain't hungry," said Johnnie. "I feel sick."

"Sick? You ain't a-going to be ill on me are yer?"

"You stole them things!" Johnnie stopped and confronted his father. "You took them off of that fat geyser!"

"Now, now . . ." said Cleaver, trying to move him along.

"You stole them from out of his pocket! I saw you!"

"You're a sharp lad, Johnnie. I *meant* you to see that. So you can learn how to do it."

"If that's your job I don't want to learn it," said Johnnie, disgustedly. He started walking away.

"Listen, Johnnie." His father hurried after him. "Listen! It's a good job what brings in twenty shillings at one go, ain't it?" He panted for breath as Johnnie was walking very fast. "Look, maybe I was wrong to take Mrs Jessop's money – she's poor. But that gent, what right 'ad he got to a gold watch like that? Why should he have 'is pockets full of money and 'is fat belly full of food and us 'ave nothing? He's full and we're starving."

"He works, Father," said Johnnie.

"Well? I works now, don't I?"

"But stealing doesn't help no one. Maybe it helps fill your pockets now, but it ain't good in the long run. It means prison, Father. That's what it means."

Cleaver stopped in his tracks, suddenly frightened. "Johnnie!" he called pathetically. "I needs your help!"

"You needs someone's help," called back Johnnie. "I heard what Mallinger said!"

"D'you know what he'd do to me if you don't play the game?" Cleaver puffed and panted after him. "And you'd let him do that? Not lift a finger to help me?"

"I didn't say I wouldn't help you Father."

Johnnie took pity on him and slowed down a bit. "You must go away!"

"Shhhhh! Not so loud!" whispered Cleaver. Their

voices echoed in the deserted alleyway. It was very quiet. From somewhere down on their left was a sound of lapping water. Johnnie sniffed the damp air. There was a smell of mud and rotting vegetation. It was getting very dark.

"Go down to the docks," he said in a low voice. "It's not far from here. Go down to the river and get on board a ship."

"They'd track me down!" whispered Cleaver.

"Not on the sea they wouldn't." Johnnie remained steadfast, looking his father in the eye and trying desperately to convince him. "We're so close! You could go now and get on a ship. One that's sailing to the other side of the world! I'll see Mallinger doesn't get on your trail." Seeing his father hesitate, he took his arm and pulled him along through the winding streets to the edge of the river.

After his father had gone Johnnie didn't know what to do. He was afraid that if he went back to Adler's Court Mallinger would track him down. He was hungry and cold, but he didn't dare go back to the Queen Street cellar and get the remains of the food. So he stayed outside in the cold, wandering from place to place. A thick yellow fog came down, and he could no longer tell where he was. He walked for a long time, and was just turning into an alleyway to look for somewhere to sit down when a hand descended on his shoulder.

"Well, well! Here's a piece of luck!" It was Ned. "You're coming along of me, young man. The master wants a word with you." He kept his hand firmly on Johnnie's shoulder and steered him along through a maze of alleys.

Almost as soon as Johnnie realised he was back in Queen Street he was pushed inside a house. He found himself in a big warm kitchen with a long table in the centre. There were several people there and Johnnie recognised Poll, who was drinking a bowl of soup.

"Hello, my little man." Johnnie saw Mallinger smiling at him from the head of the table. "And where's your Dad, then?"

Johnnie looked at the floor.

"I found him down near Blackfriars," Ned released Johnnie and sat down at the table with a groan. "But there's no sign of Cleaver. My bones are aching with the cold." An ancient man with a bent back hobbled over from the fire and brought Ned a bowl of soup. The smell made Johnnie feel quite faint with hunger.

"Bring a bowl of soup for the young man, cookie," said Mallinger. The old man brought a steaming bowlful and set it on the table in front of Johnnie.

"Now then," said Mallinger in a friendly tone, "what's all this about your Daddy? You just tell us all about him and then you can sit down and drink your soup."

Johnnie swallowed and said nothing. He felt a rush of cold air behind him, and knew that someone had opened the door to come in. He made a dash for it. In two seconds he was flat on his face on the floor, as the man who had come in put out a leg to trip him up. Several people sitting around the room laughed. The man shoved Johnnie back towards Mallinger.

"Stand up straight when you talk to the master!" he said, hitting Johnnie between the shoulder blades.

"Where's your father, boy?" said Mallinger.

"I ain't a-going to tell!"

Everybody laughed at Johnnie except Poll, who had stopped drinking her soup and was watching him intently.

"No one says no to me," said Mallinger with a grin. "I want your father. I want him here with me, not running around with that big mouth of his telling the police about us. So you'd better tell me nicely where he's hopped it to."

Johnnie looked around at the circle of grinning faces in

the firelight. Everyone was looking at him. Most of them were smiling. Poll was not, but she looked away quickly when Johnnie caught her eye.

"You ain't got no friends here, boy. So speak up quick and save us bother." Mallinger's face was grim now. When Johnnie stayed silent he beckoned to the man who had tripped him up.

"All yours," he said.

Johnnie cried out in pain as the man's heavy leather belt came down across his shoulders. The man hit him several times. Poll jumped to her feet.

"Tell what you know, boy, and be done with it," she shouted. "There's too many of them."

Johnnie shook his head. Poll came round and whispered to him. "Look . . . you can eat your fill if you just speak up." She held up the bowl of soup.

"Stand back, Poll," warned Mallinger.

"But Cleaver's a stupid, clumsy fellow!" she said. "We can find him without the boy. He'll be no use to us if you break his bones. Swear him in and be done with it." Ned was nodding, and even Mallinger looked as if he could see some sense in what she said.

Johnnie licked his dry lips and plucked up his courage to say what he had to say. "I won't be no thief," he said.

The man slapped his face so hard that tears sprang into his eyes from the pain.

"We don't use that word here," said Mallinger coldly. Ned got up from the table and spoke quietly to Johnnie: "We could kill a little lad like you in the twinkling of an eye and not even notice the doing of it."

"I won't be a thief!" said Johnnie desperately. "Kill me if you like! But I can't do it! I can't let my mother and Alison be ashamed of me."

At a sign from Mallinger the man with the belt hit Johnnie again, and Ned took a heavy stick and began to beat him too. Johnnie heard Poll cry out in protest, then the stick caught him on the arm, and the pain was so intense it made him feel sick. There was a roaring in his ears and the bright firelight in the kitchen disappeared behind a grey mist. The shouting and laughter of the thieves grew fainter and fainter.

Chapter Eleven

Johnnie awoke to the sound of dripping water. He was in darkness, except for a little ray of light that filtered through a grating above his head. It threw a circle of light on to a dirty brick wall, glistening with water. Johnnie tried to sit up to find out where he was, but immediately fell back with a cry of pain. He was so sore and stiff he could hardly move, and the pain in his arm was the worst he had ever felt.

A door banged open and shut above his head, and a flickering pool of candle-light appeared. Johnnie turned his head with difficulty and saw two shadowy figures approaching.

"Open them pretty eyes and sit up!" said a voice in the gloom, close to his ear. It was Ned. Johnnie could not move. Poll knelt down beside him. She had a mug of water in her hand. She lifted Johnnie's head and put the mug to his lips.

"Playing the little mother, eh?" said Ned sarcastically. Johnnie sipped the water gratefully and winced as Poll leaned against his arm.

"I think his arm's broke!" she said.

"There'll be more than his arm broke if he don't come round to our way of thinking." Ned looked down at Johnnie. "Now listen to me, little Cleaver. If you behaves yourself when we takes you up to see the master tomorrow then we'll fix up your arm all comfy and you'll want for nothing."

Johnnie shook his head weakly and shut his eyes. Ned continued: "Our Mallinger looks after his own. He looks after them well – look at the fat on me and Poll." He pinched Poll's cheek, then put his face down close to Johnnie's so that Johnnie could smell his beery breath:

"You got till tomorrow night. I'm fond of you. You got spunk. So don't let me down." He got up. "Come on, Poll. Let's get outa' here. It gives me the creeps." He hurried to the door, taking the candle with him. "And if you don't come round to our way of thinking," he called, "then we can always knock you on the head, and dump you in the river, and your precious Alison won't even know you've gone."

"Johnnie . . ." whispered Poll in the darkness, "I can't a-bear this . . ."

"Don't worry," said Johnnie hoarsely, "I reckon I'll be dead by tomorrow night."

"No you won't," whispered Poll. "What they done to you last night don't kill. They're too clever for that. But I can't a-bear to think of them hurting you again or putting you in the river."

"If I'm dead they can't hurt me no more . . ."

"There'll be others," Poll sighed in the darkness.

"Others?" said Johnnie.

"Boys are always coming and going. Sometimes girls too. I can't a-bear it no more, I can't!" Johnnie heard Poll moving restlessly. "I don't know what to do," she muttered. "I'm afraid of them. I can't get you out of here, we'd be seen! But I must do something." She knelt down again beside him. "Here, eat some of this bread. You must try to keep your strength up." The door opened with a crash.

"Poll, come out of there," yelled Ned.

"Johnnie, where d'you live?" she whispered quickly. Johnnie scarcely heard her. His eyes were closing. "Johnnie – quickly – where does your mother live?"

"Poll?" shouted Ned impatiently.

"Mother?" Johnnie groaned and opened his eyes.

"Where does she live?" Poll pinched his good arm to wake him up.

"Oh – Adler's Court, number four."

"Adler's Court," whispered Poll, and slipped away as Ned yelled for her again.

It was beginning to get dark in the courtyard. Bess, Alison and some other girls were skipping with a long rope.

All in together girls,
This fine weather girls,
When I count to twenty
This rope must be empty,
Five, ten, fifteen, twenty!

They all sang together, and when they got to the end of the song they all ran out of the rope and got ready to start again, one by one running in until they were all jumping the rope together. Alison was turning one handle of the rope, for it needed a steady hand to keep the rhythm going with so many girls jumping the rope at once.

Jos sat watching them from the doorstep, with the baby propped beside him. The baby was getting bigger and stronger, and could sit up quite well now.

Mrs Jessop came out of the house and picked up the baby for a moment. She stayed until the skipping game was over, then she called to Alison: "I'm just off! I won't be long."

Alison ran over to kiss her goodbye, and was just going to rejoin the game when she heard a hoarse voice whispering her name: "Alison!" She looked all round, but could see no one. Then a tall ragged girl with a shawl wrapped round her beckoned from the dark alleyway. "Come quickly," she whispered. It was Poll.

"Is your name Cleaver?" she asked, as soon as they were safely in the shadows. Alison shook her head. Poll looked behind her quickly as if she was afraid of being followed. "Do you know someone called Cleaver? Johnnie Cleaver?" she asked impatiently.

"Oh – do you know where he is?" asked Alison eagerly.

"Shhhhh!" said Poll. "Keep your voice down! I daren't be seen."

"Tell me where he is."

"It's a long way from here. Queen Street. Near the river. Is his mother in the house?"

"Yes." Alison nodded.

"Listen careful, then. I don't want no police in on this." Poll took Alison's arm and pulled her further into the shadows.

"Is Johnnie all right?"

"Shhhh . . . he's in danger."

"What?"

"Bring his mother here. Don't tell no one else. Just bring her here, fast."

Alison nodded. She ran out of the alley and into the kitchen as fast as she could. For once it was quite peaceful in there, with all the children outside playing. Mrs Cleaver was busy ironing.

"If it's anything to do with that baby, I don't want to know," she called as Alison ran in.

"No, no," said Alison. "A person wants to see you."

"A person?" said Mrs Cleaver. "Has our Bess been up to something?"

"It's about Johnnie!"

Mrs Cleaver put the iron back on its resting place by the fire and wiped her hands on her apron. She hurried out into the courtyard after Alison. They went to the alley, but there was no sign of anyone there. A policeman had strolled into the courtyard and was watching the skipping game with great enjoyment. Alison ran up and down the alley.

"She's gone!"

Mrs Cleaver's face fell. "Are you sure you wasn't dreaming it up, Alison?"

"I saw her!"

"I know you want Johnnie back, but . . ."

"She spoke to me!"

"Well she ain't a-speaking now." Mrs Cleaver sighed and made her way slowly back to the kitchen. "Don't be playing these tricks on me gal. I ain't up to them."

"But she spoke to me! He's in Queen Street, she said!"

Mrs Cleaver ignored her. "What with one thing and another . . ." she muttered, and called to Bess; Bess pulled a face and left the skipping game reluctantly.

"Cheer up, you'll soon be dead!" she said rudely, seeing Alison's unhappy face.

"Bess, wait a minute," said Alison. "Do you know where Queen Street is?"

"It's down by the river. I been there once with Father." Bess pulled an even more unpleasant face at the memory. "I thought we was going to see the Queen. Oh my – it's a terrible place! Much worse than here. He told me not to tell no one. He was a-selling something to someone. They said they'd buy me off of him, so I ran like hell!" She laughed and headed for the kitchen. "What d'you want with Queen Street anyway?"

"Johnnie's there!"

"Oh my eyes!" Bess's mouth dropped open. "Father's took 'im there! He'll have sold him. That's it, Father's sold him!" Bess shivered.

"Can you take me there?" asked Alison.

"I can, but you might never come back," said Bess.

"Bess, get in here and fold this laundry!" came a shout from the kitchen.

"Can we go now?" asked Alison.

"Go now?" Bess was amazed. "Not till I done this rotten laundry. And not if you're wearing that dress. They'll have it off your back before you can say Jack Robinson!" Bess turned to go in and saw the policeman.

"Why don't you tell that bobby?" she asked.

"No, I can't. He won't believe me. Your mother didn't believe me . . ." Alison looked up at the policeman and went very red. He smiled at her and gave a friendly wave as he made his way out of the courtyard. He looked so strong and reliable that Alison nearly ran after him and told him everything. But she decided against it, and went upstairs to get ready.

Chapter Twelve

"Poll! You ain't brought nothing in today." Mallinger was in the warm kitchen of the thieves' house. He was admiring himself in a small mirror that hung on the wall. Poll crouched on a low stool by the fire and hugged her knees. "Ain't you feeling well?" Mallinger licked his forefinger and slicked down his moustache. He surveyed the result in the mirror with pleasure.

"I'm well."

"Then give over staring into the fire and make a drop of coffee!" Poll got up listlessly and moved the great iron kettle on to the fire.

"You look like you got a load on your mind," said Mallinger.

"She's sweet on little Cleaver!" said Ned, looking up from a pile of stolen wallets he was emptying.

"Oh well," Mallinger grinned. "In that case you can do the whacking Poll, when we get him up here tomorrow."

"Why can't you let him go?" she burst out. "He's only a child."

"Playing the little mother, eh?" Mallinger's grin widened. "No, we'll keep him here just for you, so you can practise your motherly instincts on him, eh Ned?" The two of them laughed.

The sound of their laughter did not reach the coal hole where Johnnie lay. Sometimes he heard footsteps passing in the street above him, but that was all. Several times during the day he had shouted for help but there had been no reply. Now it was getting dark, and he hardly knew where he was any more. He kept falling into a doze, in which he imagined all kinds of things.

"Alison!" he murmured. "Father's gone to be a sailor!" He moved his head restlessly on the damp floor. "Shall I be a sailor? Where's the trumpet? The silver trumpet?"

At Adler's Court, Alison was struggling into an old dress which was now too small for her. She had unfastened her usually neat hair and run her fingers through it to make it tangled, and looked in the mirror to see the final effect. It was all right, but her face looked very white and clean. She grabbed some soot from inside the chimney, and smudged it over her face and hands. Then she took the bosun's call and hurried down to the courtyard. It was very dark now. No children were playing, but Bess was standing by the lamp-post.

"You ready then?" she said. "I thought you was joking!"

"No," said Alison.

"You look like a chimney sweep!" Bess wiped Alison's face with the hem of her dress. "You're much too dirty."

Alison was anxious to get away, but Bess was reluctant. "Listen, I can't get mixed up in nothing. We ought to tell someone first."

"No!" cried Alison. "She said not to! Let's find Johnnie first." They scurried off through the dark streets.

Mrs Jessop was very surprised to find the room empty when she arrived home with Jim and a basket of supper.

"Did you see Alison down in the courtyard?" she asked. "She was there when I left. And look, she's let the fire go down!"

"Here, let me." Jim took the coal scuttle from her and put some coals on the fire. "She's playing a bit further afield maybe."

"But she never forgets the fire!"

Jim could see that Mrs Jessop was very worried. So, after they had sat for a while waiting for Alison, and she still did not appear, he went downstairs to have a word with Mrs Cleaver.

It was the Cleavers' supper-time. All the children were standing round a small table as there were not enough chairs for them to sit on. Mrs Cleaver was trying to serve up the stew and balance the baby on her arm at the same time. All the children were talking and shouting and the baby was crying, so Jim had some trouble making himself heard. Eventually Mrs Cleaver realised what he was trying to tell her.

"I ain't seen Alison, and I ain't seen my Bess either. Not for a good hour," she said over the clamour.

"It's not like Alison to go off and not say," Jim said, and took the baby from her.

"Thank you very much," said Mrs Cleaver, wielding her ladle with much more ease. "I need five pairs of hands I do! That Alison's took to wandering off a lot since Johnnie went. She's looking for him."

"But not so late, surely!" said Jim.

"Look, she's left her dress!" Mrs Jessop came into the kitchen looking quite distraught and clutching Alison's dress.

"She's not gone out naked surely!" said Mrs Cleaver, dropping the ladle. "Oh my Gawd! I hope our Bess hasn't got her up to mischief."

"Which house is it, Bess?" asked Alison in the quietest whisper she could manage. They were pressed against the wall at the end of Queen Street. Sounds of singing and shouting came from further up the street.

Bess shook her head. "I don't remember."

"You must remember! Try!" But Bess had no idea which house her father had taken her to so long ago. Alison was almost in despair. She could not go knocking on doors and asking if Johnnie was inside. The rowdy noises echoing down the street did not sound welcoming at all. Then suddenly she remembered the bosun's call.

"You ain't a-going to blow that!" Bess was horrified. "I ain't a-coming with you if you do." But Alison had already slipped away, the trumpet in her hand.

Poll was down in the cellar with Johnnie when he heard the first faint sound from the bosun's call. He started and grabbed her hand. He tried to whistle, but his lips were too dry. "Water!" he croaked. Poll gave him a drink, and when Alison blew again he was able to answer with a faint whistle.

Alison was standing by the grating. She was about to walk on down the street when she heard Johnnie's whistle. For a moment she could not work out where it was coming from. Then she noticed the grating by her feet, and realised that Johnnie must be down below in the cellar. She knelt down and pressed her face close to the grating. "What shall I do, Johnnie?" she whispered. She could hear nothing from the depths of the cellar except Johnnie's very faint whistle. She spoke louder.

Suddenly the house door burst open and Ned half fell on to the pavement. "Lor, a silly girl!" he said, peering at her in the darkness. Alison sprang up, but even though he was very drunk Ned's reactions were quicker. He grabbed her and lifted her right off her feet.

"You'll be whistling a different tune in a minute," he said with a drunken laugh.

At that precise moment, Bess, who'd been watching from a safe distance, took to her heels. She remembered Ned, and the memory was not a pleasant one. She was not in a hurry to meet him again, and ran back to Adler's Court as fast as she could.

"Can't I have no peace?" sighed Mrs Cleaver, who had just sat down by the fire with her feet up. Bess was completely out of breath. She could not speak, but stood bent double, trying to recover from her long run.

"Is it about Alison?" said Jim, who was still waiting in the kitchen. Bess stood with her sides heaving and nodded her head.

"Speak up Bess, tell us."

"She's been took . . ."

"Took?" Mrs Cleaver's feet came down from the fender at once.

"And they've got our Johnnie too . . ."

"Where are they, Bess?"

"Queen Street."

"The thieves' den!" Mrs Cleaver went pale. Jim got to his feet. He asked Bess which house in Queen Street, then he said: "Righty-ho mates, all hands on deck!" and hurried out.

"Ohhh!" Johnnie moaned with the pain in his arm. He was propped up between Alison and Poll in a corner of the kitchen. The big table where the men were playing cards was between them and the door.

Only Ned was bothering with them. The rest of the thieves had got bored with the episode. "Three little beggars in a tub, tub, tub . . ." said Ned with a leer.

"My game I think," said Mallinger, immaculate as ever. He threw down his last card and collected a handful of money from his opponent.

"What you up to?" exclaimed the man resentfully.

"You oughter keep your eyes on the game sonny," said Mallinger, slipping the money into the pocket of his striped suit. Suddenly he froze.

"It's a cat, Mall," said Ned, noticing his boss's face. "You're gettin' nervous!"

"Bigger feet than a cat." Mallinger rose to his feet warily and took hold of his heavy walking stick. The other men followed his example, picking up whatever was to hand that could be used as a weapon.

"You just got nervous with that whistling, master," said Ned.

Mallinger ignored him and remained alert. After a few minutes when nothing happened he began to relax. "You're right, Neddy. Give us a game of cards . . ."

He was about to start dealing the cards when the door burst open and two policemen strode in.

"Uncle Jim!" cried Alison, who could see Jim coming in behind them. "Be careful!"

Mallinger was reaching for a long vicious-looking knife. Jim saw Alison, then saw the knife, and leapt for Mallinger, knocking it out of his hand. The other thieves put up a bit of a fight, hurling crockery at the policemen and swearing, but they soon lost heart when they saw Mallinger overpowered.

"Allie!" Uncle Jim came across and picked Alison up, trying to shield her from the fighting.

"Uncle Jim –" she cried, peering round the bulk of his body. "Stop them, please!"

Two policemen had hold of Poll and were trying to drag her away. She was biting and kicking wildly. "She was kind to Johnnie – she told me where he was – oh Uncle Jim!" But before Jim could make a move, Poll had broken free. She ran across the room to Johnnie, who had half-fainted and was lying on the floor.

"Poor boy," she said, lifting his head. "Oh you poor boy!"

Jim signalled to the policemen to leave her alone. He went over to Johnnie.

"Careful, I think his arm's broke," said Poll. At that moment Mallinger was dragged past by a policeman. He aimed a vicious kick at Poll. Jim quickly pulled her out of the way, and Alison put her arms round her protectively.

"Don't worry," she said. "Uncle Jim is here now. He'll see you're all right."

Chapter Thirteen

Several weeks later Alison looked back on that night as if it had been a terrible dream. It was hard to believe, now that she was back by the sea again, in the spring sunshine, that such a place as Queen Street could ever exist. But Johnnie was there with her in the cottage, and his pale face and bandaged arm proved that it had not been a dream.

"I love this room," he said, looking around him. Alison sighed. The living-room of the cottage was not the same as it had been when they left, it still looked quite bare. But they had managed to get a table, and a little truckle bed for Johnnie, and the shells were once more in their place on the mantelshelf.

"I never thought we'd come back," said Alison. "And I never thought my friends would be able to come too." She looked out of the little window. Down on the beach, Poll was carrying the Cleaver baby. She looked quite a different person. Her straggly hair was freshly washed and brushed, and it blew out behind her in the breeze. Her tattered old dress had been changed for a bright muslin, and her cheeks glowed with health.

"And fancy mother coming too," said Johnnie. He leaned back contentedly on his pillow and gazed out of the window. "I think this must be the most beautiful place in the world."

"It is," agreed Alison.

"Bess, come out 'ere and fold these sheets!" came a shout from outside. Mrs Cleaver was struggling to get the washing off the line in the strong wind.

"There's still washing to be done!" said Johnnie, laughing. "But at least the sun is shining."

Jim and Mrs Jessop came in from the garden with a cabbage and some potatoes.

"How's that knitting, Alison?" asked Jim.

"I hope it will be finished soon," replied Alison, looking at the long piece of knitting in her lap.

"What is it?" asked Johnnie.

"It's a seaman's jersey, for you when you go to sea."

"It looks more like a giant's sock with holes in," said Johnnie, very surprised.

"Now there's no need to be rude!" said Jim with a chuckle. "You might be needing it very soon."

"What?"

"Well now, me lucky lad, are you going to be fit in a month's time?"

"I think so," replied Johnnie. "Why?"

"Because there's a ship sailing then as needs a cabin boy."

"A cabin boy?" said Johnnie.

"That's right. And I reckon you're the boy to do it."

Johnnie fell back on his pillow and stared at Jim in amazement. "I don't believe it!"

"It's as true as I'm sitting here."

"Uncle Jim, you're a magician!" Alison clasped her knitting excitedly and dropped four stitches.

"If I am it's news to me."

"But you got us our cottage back, and now you've found a ship for Johnnie!"

Johnnie was so excited he was all for leaping out of bed at once, but Mrs Jessop stopped him. "Now then, you mustn't get excited," she said. "You've just had a nasty fever."

"How can he help getting excited?" cried Alison, and they all laughed.

"Mrs Jessop?" It was Mrs Cleaver sticking her head round the door, all flushed and wind-blown from being out in the open air. "May I come in?" She was holding a crumpled letter in her hand.

"Why yes. What's the matter?"

Mrs Cleaver sniffed. She had clearly been crying. "Cleaver's in prison," she said. "They must've caught up with him in the end." She wiped her eyes on the hem of her apron.

"Oh dear," said Mrs Jessop.

"He deserves it," said Mrs Cleaver. She blew her nose.

"Poor Father!" said Johnnie.

"Let's hope it won't be for very long," said Mrs Jessop, kindly.

"Maybe he'll come out a better man," said Mrs Cleaver.

"Mother – I'm to go to sea!" said Johnnie eagerly.

"I know, I know." Mrs Cleaver sighed. "Uncle Jim told me. I shall miss you, but there it is. Comes to us all in the end – the little birds must leave the nest." She wiped her eyes again and went back to her washing.

"I will be coming home Mother!" called Johnnie after her.

As the spring weather grew warmer, Johnnie grew steadily stronger until he was able to run about outside, with Alison and the others.

"It's lovely having you here," she said one day, as they were flying Johnnie's kite on the beach. "It was quite lonely sometimes before."

They stopped for a moment, out of breath, and Poll ran past them, snatching the kite and racing off with it to keep it in the air. Little Jos ran after her, straining his short legs to keep up.

"Johnnie, this is for you." Alison took the bosun's call out of her pocket.

"The little silver trumpet!"

"Mammy said I could give it to you now you are to be a sailor."

Johnnie took it and blew a clear note. Then he gave it

back to Alison. "Will you keep it for me, Allie?" he said. "Till I get to be a real bosun?" Alison blew the loudest note she could, and it echoed round them as they stood looking out to sea.

"It saved my life!" said Johnnie, grinning. He put his arm round Alison's shoulders, and they set off along the beach after the others.